D0206939

an **IGNATIAN** book of days

Other Books by Jim Manney

Charged with Grandeur: The Book of Ignatian Inspiration

God Finds Us: An Experience of the Spiritual Exercises of St. Ignatius Loyola

A Simple, Life-Changing Prayer: Discovering the Power of St. Ignatius Loyola's Examen

What's Your Decision? How to Make Choices with Confidence and Clarity (with J. Michael Sparough, SJ, and Tim Hipskind, SJ)

an **IGNATIAN** book of days

Daily Reflections from the Spiritual Wisdom of St. Ignatius of Loyola

JIM MANNEY

LOYOLAPRESS.
A JESUIT MINISTRY
Chicago

LoyolaPress.
A Jesuit Ministry
3441 N. Ashland Avenue
Chicago, Illinois 60657
(800) 621-1008
www.loyolapress.com

© 2014 Jim Manney
All rights reserved.

Copyright acknowledgments appear in the back of the book and constitute a continuation of this copyright page.

Cover art credit: Qweek/iStock/ThinkStock.

ISBN-13: 978-0-8294-4145-1
ISBN-10: 0-8294-4145-X
Library of Congress Control Number: 2014943764

Printed in the United States of America.

15 16 17 18 19 Versa 10 9 8 7 6 5 4 3 2

Preface

You might say there's something inevitable about this book. I am a Jesuit-educated editor and writer who has had a long career in Catholic publishing. I've come to know Ignatian spirituality well through my work for a Jesuit publishing company. I've edited many Ignatian texts and written a few. (My favorite is *A Simple, Life-Changing Prayer,* a little book about Ignatius's daily examen.) Over the years I've stuffed hundreds of quotes, excerpts, prayers, Web pages, and links into various folders on my hard drive and in the cloud. So why not pull the best of this material together and publish it—the greatest Ignatian hits, a top-365 list?

But there's also something unexpected about this book. It didn't have to happen, and it certainly didn't have to take the form it did. It's personal. At a certain point (exactly when is hard to pin down), my professional engagement with Ignatian spirituality shifted to a deep personal connection. I grew to love it. I began to see things through an Ignatian lens. My thinking changed. I have different priorities now, a different sense of what's meaningful, a different way of praying, a different way of being in the world. I've become very interested in understanding the spiritual outlook that has brought this about. What is this Ignatian "lens" that has made such a difference to me?

This book is an effort to answer that question. I suppose I answer it the way you'd think an editor would—with a great flurry of compilation, selection, arrangement, and editing. I don't try to define the Ignatian point of view. Rather, I try to share it. I wanted to find the most compelling Ignatian voices and let them speak for themselves. I'll let Ignatius Loyola and the many great thinkers, writers, and saints who followed in his footsteps show you what Ignatian spirituality is.

Ignatius had a lot to say about making good choices, so, fittingly enough, I'll say a few things about the choices I made in compiling this book.

A priority for me is to present material that will help you with prayer and reflection. Prayer isn't the only concern. Ignatian writers have had a lot to say about society, the church, human psychology, relationships, communication, and many other topics; you'll see much of that here. But with every selection, I've tried to include something that will help you pray and reflect on your experience. To assist this, with each reading I've included either a Scripture passage or my own brief reflection, as well as a question, suggestion, or prayer to get you started.

I also want this book to deepen your understanding of Ignatian spirituality. I've included many selections from the *Spiritual Exercises* and many quotes that explain and interpret the major themes of the Ignatian perspective as it has developed over the past five centuries. I've inserted some history too. You'll find entries about Jesuit saints and other notable figures, as well as major dates in Jesuit history.

I've drawn on many sources: Jesuits and laypeople, books and journals, Web pages, and blogs. I've tried to represent the entire five-century range of the Ignatian tradition, but it's fair to say that my selections are weighted toward the beginning of that tradition and the end of it. I paid special attention to Ignatius and the early Jesuits, particularly Ignatius himself, because that's where the tradition begins and finds its classic expression. I'm also especially interested in contemporary Ignatian voices. A major figure here is Pope Francis, the most famous Jesuit in the world, who is going about his work with a distinctively Ignatian attitude.

What is the Ignatian "lens" that colors and sharpens my vision? It's a conviction that we can find God in all things, that our personal experience can provide authentic knowledge of God, that Christ beckons us to join him in his work of saving and healing the world, that God is an endless giver of gifts, that the inner life of the heart and our feelings reveal the leadings of God. It's a way of seeing and thinking and praying. I hope what you read here will help you on the Ignatian way.

Jim Manney

January 1

Titular Feast of the Society of Jesus

January 1 is the titular feast of the Jesuits—that is, the feast that celebrates the order's name, the "Society of Jesus." January 1 is the day—eight days after Jesus' birth—when "it was time to circumcise the child, and he was called Jesus" (Luke 2:21). In 2013, Pope Francis talked about the Society's name:

> *In the autumn of 1537, on his way to Rome with a group of his first companions, [Ignatius] wondered,* If people ask us who we are, how should we answer? *The answer came spontaneously:* We shall say that we are the "Society of Jesus." *This demanding name intends to suggest a relationship of very close friendship and of total affection for Jesus, in whose footsteps they wanted to follow. Why have I told you about this event? Because St. Ignatius and his companions had realized that Jesus was teaching them how to live well, how to live a life that had profound meaning, that imparted enthusiasm, joy, and hope. They had understood that Jesus is a great teacher of life and a model of life, and that he was not only teaching them but also inviting them to follow him on this path.*
>
> —In *The Church of Mercy*

> Jesus said to him, "I am the way, and the truth, and the life. No one comes to the Father except through me."
>
> —John 14:6

Lord Jesus Christ, Son of God, have mercy on me, a sinner.

January 2

Why Am I Here?

Man is created to praise, reverence, and serve God our Lord, and by this means to save his soul.

The other things on the face of the earth are created for man to help him in attaining the end for which he is created.

Hence, man is to make use of them in as far as they help him in the attainment of his end, and he must rid himself of them in as far as they prove a hindrance to him.

Therefore, we must make ourselves indifferent to all created things, as far we are allowed free choice and are not under any prohibition. Consequently, as far as we are concerned, we should not prefer health to sickness, riches to poverty, honor to dishonor, a long life to a short one. The same holds for all other things.

Our one desire and choice should be what is more conducive to the end for which we are created.

—*The Spiritual Exercises* 23

The First Principle and Foundation, at the beginning of the Spiritual Exercises, expresses an idea at the heart of the Ignatian perspective: that we love and serve God and others by using the things of the world wisely.

A question for prayer: what's your purpose in life?

January 3

There God Is

Wherever space is really left by parting, by death, by renunciation, by apparent emptiness—provided that the emptiness is not filled by the world, or activity, or chatter, or the deadly grief of the world—there God is.

—Karl Rahner, SJ, *Biblical Homilies*

Emptiness is only "apparent." God is in it. But note the phrase "provided that . . ." We find God there only if we don't rush to fill the emptiness with something else.

Holy Spirit, take me to the place where God is, deep in the stillness.

January 4

Let Your Feelings Have Their Say

So allow your feelings and your moods to have their say. If you have feelings of tenderness or apprehension or anger in the situation of your scene, this is telling you something about what is happening between you and God at that particular moment. . . . [Y]our feelings and reactions in your relationship with God are very significant, even if at times they may appear to be negative. We often learn more from our negative reactions than from the more comfortable ones . . .

—Margaret Silf, *Inner Compass*

O Lord, do not rebuke me in your anger,
  or discipline me in your wrath.
Be gracious to me, O Lord, for I am languishing;
  O Lord, heal me, for my bones are shaking with terror.
My soul also is struck with terror,
  while you, O Lord—how long?
Turn, O Lord, save my life;
  deliver me for the sake of your steadfast love.

—Psalm 6:1–4

What are you worried about? What causes you anxiety? Talk to God about these feelings.

January 5

Place Your Whole Confidence in God

[P]lace your whole confidence in God through Jesus Christ; abandon yourself more and more entirely to Him, in all, and for all, and you will find by your own experience that He will always come to your assistance when you require His help. He will become your Master, your Guide, your Support, your Protector, your invincible Upholder. Then nothing will be wanting to you because, possessing God, you possess all, and to possess Him you have but to apply to Him with the greatest confidence, to have recourse to Him for everything great and small without any reserve, and to speak to Him with the greatest simplicity in this way: "Lord, what shall I do on such an occasion? What shall I say? Speak, Lord, I am listening; I abandon myself entirely to You; enlighten me, lead me, uphold me, take possession of me."

—Jean-Pierre de Caussade, SJ, *Abandonment to Divine Providence*

I am the vine, you are the branches. Those who abide in me and I in them bear much fruit, because apart from me you can do nothing.

—John 15:5

Speak to the Lord "with greatest simplicity": what shall I do today?

January 6

Do You Want to Want It?

Sometimes in Jesuit life, you might find yourself lacking the desire for something that you want to desire. *Let's say you are living in a comfortable Jesuit community and have scant contact with the poor. You may say, "I know I'm* supposed *to want to live simply and work with the poor, but I have no desire to do this." Or perhaps you know that you* should *want to be more generous, more loving, more forgiving, but don't desire it. How can you pray for that with honesty?*

In reply, Ignatius would ask, "Do you have the desire for this desire?" *Even if you don't want it, do you want to want it? Do you wish that you were the kind of person that wanted this? Even this can be seen as an invitation from God. It is a way of glimpsing God's invitation even in the faintest traces of desire.*

—James Martin, SJ, "Advent and Desire: A Meditation," *America*

Useful advice: I *should* be more disciplined, more available, more generous, but I don't desire it. But I can *want* to want it.

Is there an appropriate change or a choice that you simply don't desire? Can you desire to have that desire?

January 7

Christ Has No Home

There are many sufferings to heal. Christ stumbles through our streets in the person of so many poor who are hungry, thrown out of their miserable lodgings because of sickness and destitution. Christ has no home! And we who have the good fortune to have one and have food to satisfy our hunger, what are we doing about it?

—St. Alberto Hurtado, SJ, "Christ Has No Home," *IgnatianSpirituality.com*

A scribe then approached and said, "Teacher, I will follow you wherever you go." And Jesus said to him, "Foxes have holes, and birds of the air have nests; but the Son of Man has nowhere to lay his head."

—Matthew 8:19–20

How do you answer Hurtado's question: what are you doing about it?

January 8

Ask for What You Want

"I should ask for what I desire"

for a growing and intense sorrow and tears for my sins. 55

for the grace not to be deaf to His call, but prompt and diligent to accomplish His most holy will. 91

for an intimate knowledge of our Lord, who has become man for me, that I may love Him more and follow Him more closely. 104

for sorrow, compassion, and shame because the Lord is going to His suffering for my sins. 193

for the grace to be glad and rejoice intensely because of the great joy and the glory of Christ our Lord. 221

for an intimate knowledge of the many blessings received, that filled with gratitude for all, I may in all things love and serve the Divine Majesty. 233

—*The Spiritual Exercises*

Ignatius urges us to pray explicitly for what we want. He believed that God places these great desires in our hearts.

Spend some time in prayer today telling the Lord about your deepest desires.

January 9

We Have Contact with Everyone

To a Jesuit who hesitated to work in the king's court, fearing for the safety of his soul:

My own opinion is that the argument based on your personal safety is not relevant. Obviously if our religious profession has no other purpose but to ensure our security, and if we were supposed to subordinate the good we do to keeping clear of danger, then we would not have to live among people and have contact with them. But according to our vocation we have contact with everyone. If we go about with our intention upright and pure, . . . Christ himself will look after us in his infinite goodness.

—St. Ignatius Loyola in *Personal Writings*, Joseph A. Munitiz, SJ

Radical trust is required of Christ's disciples. There are times when we must override our own well-founded misgivings about a course of action and plunge in, trusting that Christ will provide for us.

What makes you fearful? Are these fears well-founded? Do they inhibit your freedom to choose God and other people?

January 10

Active Passivity

Our response to God is a response. *God initiates; we answer. We do not strike out on our own. We are to "follow." To follow means that we adopt a kind of active passivity toward the action of God. "Active passivity" captures the characteristic tone of Ignatian spirituality. It is a spirituality of attentiveness, of watching and waiting, of noticing the ebb and flow of our feelings and inner dispositions.*

—David L. Fleming, SJ, *What Is Ignatian Spirituality?*

As the eyes of servants
  look to the hand of their master,
as the eyes of a maid
  to the hand of her mistress,
so our eyes look to the LORD our God.

—Psalm 123:2

What have you heard God saying lately about the work you do, your commitments, the way you spend your time and money?

January 11

Everywhere There Is Good to Be Done

While staying in inns, I have always felt inspired to do good by instructing and encouraging people. It is very good to leave in the inns and houses where we happen to stay some trace of good and holy behavior; for everywhere there is good to be done, everywhere there is something to be planted and harvested. For we are indebted to all men in every condition and in every place.

—St. Peter Faber, SJ, in *The Ignatian Tradition*, Kevin F. Burke, Eileen Burke-Sullivan, Phyllis Zagano

"We are indebted to all men in every condition and in every place"—what a generous spirit! For Faber, every person he met was a gift.

Today see the people you meet with Peter Faber's eyes—as gifts to you.

January 12

"Do Something and Do It Very Well"

Be grateful. Be grateful for your talents and gifts because they are the raw material out of which you will conceive and shape your life's purpose. Whoever we are, whatever our circumstances, we can, as Archbishop Oscar Romero once put it, "do something and do it very well," whether that is raising children, teaching them to read, keeping the streets safe for them, creating dignified jobs for their parents, erecting buildings that will safely shelter them, or thinking and praying benevolent thoughts for their future.

Be grateful because gratitude is what energizes and motivates us to pursue great purpose.

—Chris Lowney, *Heroic Living*

I thank you that you have answered me
  and have become my salvation.
The stone that the builders rejected
  has become the chief cornerstone.
This is the LORD's doing;
  it is marvelous in our eyes.
This is the day that the LORD has made;
  let us rejoice and be glad in it.

—Psalm 118:21–24

Ignatius said, "Ask for interior knowledge of all the great good we have received, in order that, stirred to profound gratitude, we may become able to love and serve."

January 13

Praying with the Imagination

Pick a story out of scripture. Read through it once slowly and put it down. Now we begin to imagine the scene as if we are standing right there. What is around me? Who else is there? What do I hear in the scene? If I am in a house, what noises are in the house or in the street outside? What are the smells I can pick up?

Now we begin to imagine the scene we read about. Who is in it? What conversation takes place? What is the mood—tense? joyful? confused? angry?

Feel free to paint this picture in any way your imagination takes you.

—"How Do We Pray With Our Imagination?" Creighton University Online Ministries

These are Gospel passages that work well for imaginative prayer: the calling of the disciples, the Transfiguration, the healing of Bartimaeus, the woman at the well, the raising of Lazarus.

Pray imaginatively with one of your favorite Gospel stories.

January 14

Looking Outward Together

I have often quoted what Antoine de Saint-Exupéry said: "Love does not consist in gazing at each other, but in looking outward together in the same direction." I wonder whether the problem today is precisely that some lovers have lost the sense that there is anything else to look at besides each other, and that when they become bored they move on.

The promise of love is like the promise of a shared pilgrimage: that of moving together toward God, and therefore toward the source of love. Only with such a hopeful promise can couples weather the inevitable storms of the pilgrimage. And only with such a promise can one sustain hope, sustain desire, sustain joy—even during periods when one is unhappy.

—Tim Muldoon, *Dot Magis* blog

> And let us consider how to provoke one another to love and good deeds, not neglecting to meet together, as is the habit of some, but encouraging one another.
>
> —Hebrews 10:24–25

Reflect on your pilgrimage—and on the people who share it with you. Consider what you share. Can you put it into words?

January 15

Nothing Is More Practical Than Finding God

Nothing is more practical than finding God, than falling in love in a quite absolute, final way. What you are in love with, what seizes your imagination, will affect everything. It will decide what will get you out of bed in the morning, what you do with your evenings, how you spend your weekends, what you read, whom you know, what breaks your heart, and what amazes you with joy and gratitude. Fall in love, stay in love, and it will decide everything.

—Pedro Arrupe, SJ

In the Ignatian view, love is very concrete. Arrupe says that it is practical. Ignatius said that love ought to be expressed in deeds rather than in words. It consists of mutual sharing.

What gets you out of bed in the morning?

January 16

Seek Grace for the Smallest Things

Seek grace for the smallest things, and you will also find grace to accomplish, to believe in, and to hope for the greatest things. Attend to the smallest things, examine them, think about putting them into effect, and the Lord will grant you greater.

—St. Peter Faber, SJ, in *The Spiritual Writings of Pierre Favre: The Memoriale and Selected Letters and Instructions*

"Well done, good and trustworthy servant; you have been trustworthy in a few things, I will put you in charge of many things; enter into the joy of your master."

—Matthew 25:21

Ask for the grace to be faithful to a small, nagging task that you find difficult to do.

January 17

Draw Fruit from Your Illnesses

Try to draw fruit from your illnesses, not only for yourself but for the edification of others. Do not be impatient or difficult to please. Rather, have and show much patience and obedience to your doctor and whoever is taking care of you. And use good and edifying words that show that the sickness is accepted as a gift from the hand of our Creator and Lord, since sickness is a gift not less than health.

—Constitutions of the Society of Jesus, n. 272

First surprise: The constitutions of the Jesuits include an exhortation about how to be a good patient. Second surprise: the advice has to do mainly with how the sick person can serve others, not himself.

How have you drawn spiritual benefit from times of sickness?

January 18

Do Good Right Now

We should never postpone a good work, no matter how small it may be, *with the thought of later doing something greater. It is a very common temptation of the enemy to be always placing before us the perfection of things to come and bring us to make little of the present. (Emphasis added.)*

—St. Ignatius Loyola, *The Letters of St. Ignatius of Loyola,* William J. Young, SJ

Resolved: I will do the good thing I can do today.

Resolve to do one good deed for someone else in the day to come.

January 19

Do You Create Unity?

We must all ask ourselves: How do I let myself be guided by the Holy Spirit in such a way that my life and my witness of faith are both unity and communion? Do I convey the word of reconciliation and of love, which is the Gospel, to the milieus in which I live? At times it seems that we are repeating today what happened at Babel: division, the incapacity to understand one another, rivalry, envy, egoism. What do I do with my life? Do I create unity around me? Or do I cause division by gossip, criticism, or envy? What do I do? Let us think about this. Spreading the Gospel means that we are the first to proclaim and live the reconciliation, forgiveness, peace, unity, and love that the Holy Spirit gives us.

—Pope Francis, *The Church of Mercy*

Now I appeal to you, brothers and sisters, by the name of our Lord Jesus Christ, that all of you should be in agreement and that there should be no divisions among you, but that you should be united in the same mind and the same purpose.

—1 Corinthians 1:10

Answer the pope's question: Do you create unity? If so, how?

January 20

Helping Souls

Service is at the core of Ignatian spirituality, encapsulated in a phrase that Ignatius used more than any other in his writings: "helping souls." . . . If, as Ignatius put it in the Jesuit constitutions, we can and ought to "seek God our Lord in all things," then there is no aspect of life or human endeavor that is outside of grace or inappropriate for Christian service.

—Ronald Modras, *Ignatian Humanism*

No aspect of life is inappropriate for Christian service. Consider the implications: teaching an aerobics class, drilling for oil, writing advertising copy. Are these areas of Christian service?

How are you "helping souls"? List the ways. Speak to God about them.

January 21

Two Warning Signals

Two phrases that we might take to heart as warning signals are if only *and* what if. *The* if onlys *of our life give us an excuse for dwelling on the past and on the unchangeable features of our circumstances. The* what ifs *have the same negative effects in the future tense. Energy spent on them is definitely negative energy that is not leading us closer to God.*

—Margaret Silf, *Inner Compass*

The past is gone. The future hasn't happened. The present moment is the moment of grace.

Where have you been bogged down in "if only" and "what if" speculation?

January 22

Love the Daily Working

"You have to love the daily working," suggested choreographer Merce Cunningham. He was talking about what it took to be a dancer. He meant you have to enjoy being crammed into a studio taking class with forty other students, that you have to delight in the doing of the hundred-thousandth plié. You have to be willing to lovingly and gratefully return to the basics each and every day, even in the midst of chaos, or you cannot dance.

—Michelle Francl-Donnay, *This Ignatian Life* blog

Love your routines—e-mail, household chores, exercise, daily prayer.

What aspects of your daily routine do you find rewarding? What aspects are tedious?

January 23

When We're Desolate, Fight Back

Though in desolation we must never change our former resolutions, it will be very advantageous to intensify our activity against the desolation. We can insist more upon prayer, upon meditation, and on much examination of ourselves. We can make an effort in a suitable way to do some penance.

—*The Spiritual Exercises* 319

When we'er feeling low, we seldom want to rouse ourselves to extra effort. But that's precisely what we need to do, according to Ignatius. Fight it. Pray more. Get active.

Is there something that you know you should do but just lack the energy to do? Talk to God about this.

January 24

Ever Open to Something New

Looking back on our lives, can any of us honestly say we knew exactly the path our lives would take? Isn't it true that God has moved about in each of our lives and surprised us with all manner of twists and turns we could not have predicted or perhaps even desired?

Ignatius reminds us that we must remain ever open to the new ways God is inviting us to live our lives. If anything impedes our ability to remain open, then we must prayerfully consider what to do. When Ignatius instructs us not to fix our desires on health over sickness, for example, he prods us to consider whether our faith allows us to trust that God can be experienced even in frailty and sickness—and that good can come of it.

—Patrick McGrath, SJ, *Partners* magazine

I am about to do a new thing;
now it springs forth, do you not perceive it?
I will make a way in the wilderness
and rivers in the desert.

—Isaiah 43:19

Lord, make me ready for the new thing that you are doing in my life.

January 25

Maxims on Friendship

"A friend is another self."

"God commands us to make friends so that we can help one another."

"Our most intimate friends are those with whom we can share our innermost feelings."

"If there were no friends in the world, there would be no joy."

—Matteo Ricci, SJ, in *Ignatian Humanism*, Ron Modras

Friendship is a great gift in the Ignatian view. The Society of Jesus emerged from a circle of close friends who gathered around Ignatius. He thought that human friendship was one of God's greatest gifts, mirroring the intimate relationship we have with God.

Who are your friends? What can you do to strengthen your friendships? Talk to God about this.

January 26

Don't Take Options Off the Table

We cannot honestly discern if from the outset we preclude morally good options or assume that God must want what we want. It is not up to us to take options off the table or insist on certain things before discernment begins. Our attitude should be this: I want only what God wants, and I'm simply trying to discover what that is. Unless we have this attitude, we are not seeking the gift God wants to give but rather are insisting on getting whatever we happen to want.

—Peter F. Ryan, SJ, "How to Discern the Elements of Your Personal Vocation"

You shall love the Lord your God with all your heart, and with all your soul, and with all your mind. This is the greatest and first commandment.

—Matthew 22:37–38

What have you taken off the table—the things you must have?

January 27

What Do I Really Want?

The question to be constantly asked in decision making is, "what do I really want?" Deep down, that's what God wants too. God wants what is best for us. This isn't something repugnant, or burdensome, or sad, or difficult. The way of life that God desires for us is the way of life we *desire.*

"What do I really want?" is a simple question, but simple isn't the same as easy. Usually this question is quite difficult to answer. Our deepest desires are obscured by pride, fears, ambitions, and attachments to money, honor, security, and a host of other things. The process of discernment is essentially a process of stripping away these false desires and finding the desires at the core of our selves.

—J. Michael Sparough, SJ, *What's Your Decision?*

Take delight in the LORD,
and he will give you the desires of your heart.

—Psalm 37:4

Ask God to make you aware of the wants and fears that are obscuring your knowledge of your deepest, truest desires.

January 28

God Is Waiting for You

God is indeed waiting for you; he asks of you only the courage to go to him. How many times in my pastoral ministry have I heard it said, "Father, I have many sins"? And I have always pleaded, "Don't be afraid, go to him, he is waiting for you, he will take care of everything." We hear many offers from the world around us; but let us take up God's offer instead: his is a caress of love. For God, we are not numbers, we are important; indeed we are the most important thing to him. Even if we are sinners, we are what is closest to his heart.

—Pope Francis, *The Church of Mercy*

So he set off and went to his father. But while he was still far off, his father saw him and was filled with compassion; he ran and put his arms around him and kissed him.

—Luke 15:20

Where do you need to experience the Father's mercy? Speak to God about it.

January 29

The "Feeling" of Feelings

In souls that are progressing to greater perfection, the action of the good angel is delicate, gentle, delightful. It may be compared to a drop of water penetrating a sponge.

The action of the evil spirit upon such souls is violent, noisy, and disturbing. It may be compared to a drop of water falling upon a stone.

—*The Spiritual Exercises* 335

This is one of Ignatius's rules for the discernment of spirits. In general—not always—a restless heart is a danger sign. If a course of action feels disturbing, take another look.

Consider this principle in connection with plans you are making. Are you disturbed about them, or are you calm and secure?

January 30

Mary Ward

Mary Ward (1585–1645), an English nun who founded a women's religious community modeled on the Jesuits, died on this day in 1645. Ward wanted to enable women to serve in active roles in the Church as men were doing in the Jesuits. Her ideas met with considerable opposition in a society accustomed to religious women serving within the walls of a monastery. Her community was even suppressed for a time, but it was revived and approved by the pope in 1703. She is regarded as the foundress of two women's religious communities—the Congregation of Jesus and the Sisters of Loreto.

She was resolute in pursuing her vision. A friend wrote of her:

What applause would she not have won, what friends would she have acquired and have made herself an object of admiration to the world, if she would have relented but a little on some points regarding the Institute. But she put herself aside, without regarding what was agreeable or disagreeable. Her only ambition being fidelity to God, which she desired so much that it did not appear difficult whatever she suffered in so doing—to lose friends and make enemies, to despise honors and embrace contempt, to reject riches and embrace poverty.

—In *The Way of Ignatius Loyola*, Philip Sheldrake

What has been your response when your plans meet opposition?

January 31

The Countercultural Gift of Christ

A Jesuit freely gives what he has freely received: the gift of Christ's redeeming love.

Today we bring this countercultural gift of Christ to a world beguiled by self-centered human fulfilment, extravagance, and soft living, a world that prizes prestige, power, and self-sufficiency. In such a world, to preach Christ poor and humble with fidelity and courage is to expect humiliation, persecution, and even death. We have seen this happen to our brothers in recent years. Yet we move forward resolutely out of our "desire to resemble and imitate in some manner our Creator and Lord Jesus Christ . . . since he is the way which leads men to life." Today, as always, it is deep, personal devotion to Jesus, himself the Way, that principally characterizes the Jesuit way of proceeding.

—Society of Jesus, Thirty-Fourth General Congregation

The path of Jesus the Way cuts against the grain of the conventional wisdom and the ordinary way of doing things, against power and pride and injustice. This is the Ignatian way.

In what circumstances are you most conscious of the countercultural side of the Gospel?

February 1

Where Can I Do the Greater Good?

Seeking the magis *in Ignatian spirituality means paying attention to means and ends and discerning what is "more conducive" to achieving the end results desired. It's a matter of discriminating between options and choosing the better of the two. Thus one prays over one's choices, looks at one's gifts, considers the needs, and then decides where one can do the greater good.*

—Ronald Modras, *Ignatian Humanism*

The *magis* also means being always open to change, always alert to the possibility that the Lord is calling you to something new.

Right now, where must you choose which of several options will bring the greater good? How will you determine the greater good?

February 2

Alfred Delp, SJ

Alfred Delp, SJ, a German Jesuit, was executed on this day in 1945 for his resistance to the Nazi regime. An expert in Catholic social teaching, he worked with underground groups to develop plans for a post-Hitler Germany. He was a gifted writer whose prison writings have been collected and published.

Shortly before his execution, he wrote:

Yet it does happen, even under these circumstances, that every now and then my whole being is flooded with pulsating life and my heart can scarcely contain the delirious joy there is in it . . .

Outwardly nothing is changed. The hopelessness of the situation remains only too obvious; yet one can face it undismayed. One is content to leave everything in God's hands. And that is the whole point. Happiness in this life is inextricably mixed with God.

—*The Prison Meditations of Father Delp*

> The farmer waits for the precious crop from the earth, being patient with it until it receives the early and the late rains. You also must be patient.
>
> —James 5:7–8

Reflect on the circumstances in your life that call for patience. Ask for the grace of patience.

February 3

Surrounded by God

May the Lord and his kingdom be above you, so that your minds may be drawn upwards; may he be within you, so that you may be truly rooted in him; may he be as a firm foundation beneath you, so that you may always rely upon him; may he be at your right side, so that he will never let you swerve to pleasures or vanities; may he be at your left, so that you may never be broken by adversity; may he be behind you, so that through fear of him you will be recalled from any backsliding onwards to your perfection. May God do all this.

—St. Peter Faber, SJ, in *The Ignatian Tradition*, Kevin F. Burke, Eileen Burke-Sullivan, Phyllis Zagano

A great prayer with an eye-catching image—God is within us and all around us, protecting, nourishing, sustaining, drawing us on.

Do your work today seeing yourself in the image of Faber's prayer—as surrounded by God.

February 4

Your Most Eloquent Statement Is Your Example

Consult your own heart and decide what kind of person you want to be. You have a brief journey on this planet—how will you treat yourself, your work, and those you meet along the way? Your values are not what you say, but how you treat people, how you run meetings, whom you hire, how you treat your child who wants to play when you come home exhausted, whether you inconvenience yourself to support your friends, and how you react in a host of other daily moments.

—Chris Lowney, *Heroic Living*

Often it's easy to overlook the small deeds, such as what we do when we come home from work. St. Ignatius said that love ought to be shown in deeds rather than in words.

If your deeds could speak, what statement did you make in the past twenty-four hours?

February 5

Pedro Arrupe, SJ

Pedro Arrupe, SJ, superior general of the Jesuits from 1965 to 1983, died on this day in 1991. Arrupe guided the Society through the tumultuous post-Vatican II years. He called for a renewed commitment to the Society's roots in the Spiritual Exercises, and he oriented the Jesuits toward service to the poor and to refugees. He had a charismatic personality and was beloved by many in the Society and outside it.

He articulated the goal of Jesuit education as training "men and women for others":

Men and women who will live not for themselves but for God and his Christ—for the God who lived and died for all the world; men and women who cannot even conceive of love of God which does not include love for the least of their neighbors; men and women completely convinced that love of God which does not issue in justice for others is a farce.

> Let love be genuine; hate what is evil, hold fast to what is good; love one another with mutual affection; outdo one another in showing honor.
>
> —Romans 12:9–10

Are you complacent, too accepting of things as they are? Talk to God about this.

February 6

St. Paul Miki, SJ

Today is the feast of St. Paul Miki, SJ (1564–1597), a Jesuit novice from a noble Japanese family who was martyred along with twenty-five companions at Nagasaki in 1597.

This is from an eyewitness account of the execution:

Our brother Paul Miki, seeing himself raised to the most honorable position that he had ever occupied, openly proclaimed that he was a Japanese and a member of the Society of Jesus. And that he was being put to death for having preached the gospel. He gave thanks to God for such a precious favor.

He then added these words: "Having arrived at this moment of my existence, I believe that no one of you thinks I want to hide the truth. That is why I declare to you that there is no other way of salvation than the one followed by Christians. Since this way teaches me to forgive my enemies and all who have offended me, I willingly forgive the king and all those who have desired my death. And I pray that they will obtain the desire of Christian baptism."

> You have heard that it was said, "You shall love your neighbor and hate your enemy." But I say to you, Love your enemies and pray for those who persecute you . . .
>
> —Matthew 5:43–44

Consider the people who dislike you, who oppose your ideas and aims. How can you show love to them?

February 7

A Saint Who Lives in Complete Activity

The Ignatian man ought to be a saint and he ought to live in complete activity. Previous spirituality opposed these two aspects. Activity seemed to be an obstacle to holiness which was conceived as contemplation. The revolution accomplished by St. Ignatius showed that that which appeared to be an obstacle could become a means. To the heart filled with God, all things speak of Him. And it is not a question merely of an orientation of the will, but of a spiritual experience where God is "tasted" in everything.

—Jean Danielou, SJ, in *Christian Spirituality*, George Lane, SJ

Finding God in action is a matter of spiritual experience more than intellectual understanding.

Lord, open the eyes of my heart to see you in the work I do today.

February 8

Ignatius's Schoolmaster

At this time God treated Ignatius just as a schoolmaster treats a little boy when he teaches him. This perhaps was because of his rough and uncultivated understanding, or because he had no one to teach him, or because of the firm will God Himself had given him in His service. But he clearly saw, and always had seen that God dealt with him like this.

—St. Ignatius Loyola in *A Pilgrim's Journey*, Joseph N. Tylenda, SJ

This comment is often quoted as an example of Ignatius's great humility. But it also shows great confidence and assurance: Ignatius thought that what he learned came directly from God.

Lord, teach me what I need to know. Give me wisdom. Let me know your mind.

February 9

What Do I Love When I Love My God?

It is not physical beauty nor temporal glory nor the brightness of light dear to earthly eyes, nor the sweet melodies of all kinds of songs, nor the gentle odor of flowers, and ointments and perfumes, nor manna or honey, nor limbs welcoming the embraces of the flesh; it is not these I love when I love my God. Yet there is a light I love, and a food, and a kind of embrace when I love my God—a light, voice, odor, food, embrace of my innerness, where my soul is floodlit by light which space cannot contain, where there is sound that time cannot seize, where there is a perfume which no breeze disperses, where there is a taste for food no amount of eating can lessen, and where there is a bond of union that no satiety can part. That is what I love when I love my God.

—St. Augustine, *Confessions*

This famous passage expresses an Ignatian paradox: God transcends the beauty and sweetness of the world, yet our experience of God is mysteriously anchored in our everyday experience.

Reflect on this passage. What do you love when you love God?

February 10

Be the Person You Actually Are

Humility consists in being precisely the person you actually are before God, and since no two people are alike, if you have the humility to be yourself you will not be like anyone else in the whole universe.

It is not humility to insist on being someone that you are not. It is as much as saying that you know better than God who you are and who you ought to be. How do you expect to arrive at the end of your own journey if you take the road to another man's city? How do you expect to reach your own perfection by leading someone else's life?

—Thomas Merton, *New Seeds of Contemplation*

"Be yourself"—so true that it's become a cliché, but it often feels easier and more exciting to try to be someone else.

What hinders you from being "the person you actually are before God"?

February 11

Idleness Breaks the Soul

For the love of God, do not be careless or tepid. For if tautness breaks the bow, idleness breaks the soul. Try to maintain a holy and discreet ardor in work and in the pursuit of learning as well as of virtue. With one as with the other, one energetic act is worth a thousand that are listless, and what a lazy man cannot accomplish in many years an energetic man usually achieves in a short time.

—St. Ignatius Loyola, *The Letters of St. Ignatius of Loyola*,
William J. Young, SJ

Here's the other side of reflective Ignatian discernment: In the end, *do something,* even if the direction isn't entirely clear. There are many ways to serve God. Don't be dead in the water. Get the ship moving.

Lord, show me how to be usefully active in the service of others. Show me how to make better use of my time.

February 12

What's Next?

St. Ignatius is the exemplar of the journeying Christian. Hardly anything turned out the way he thought it would when he undertook it. He thought he should live a life of penance and austerity. That was a wrong direction. He went to the Holy Land thinking he would live his life there. He was sent home. He set out on a career as a lay evangelist. The church stopped him. He thought the Jesuits should live unencumbered by commitments, ready to go anywhere They wound up running a vast network of schools.

With all these false starts, why is Ignatius regarded as the master of discernment? Because he saw that the journey is the thing. He called himself "the pilgrim." He travelled a long way, and at every step he was alert to the still small voice pointing him to what's next.

That's the thing to think about: "What's next?"

—Jim Manney, *Dot Magis* blog

"[T]his one thing I do: forgetting what lies behind and straining forward to what lies ahead, I press on towards the goal for the prize of the heavenly call of God in Christ Jesus. Let those of us then who are mature be of the same mind."

—Philippians 3:13–15

Reflect on the question: what's next? What comes to mind?

February 13

Growing in Reverence

Ignatius believed that anyone who prayerfully considers the basic truth that we are created out of love by a transcendent God of holiness will grow in a sense of reverence. We will have a deepened sense of the sacredness of all things if we think of everything as continually being called and sustained in being by God. We will stand in awe not just before sunsets and mountains, flowers and trees, but also, and especially, before every person we meet. Reverence is a disposition of a heart that allows us to live before the beauty and goodness of every creature and the God who made them. In Ignatian terminology, reverence will enable us to find God in all things.

—Gerald M. Fagin, SJ, *Putting on the Heart of Christ*

Since we are receiving a kingdom that cannot be shaken, let us give thanks, by which we offer to God an acceptable worship with reverence and awe; for indeed our God is a consuming fire.

—Hebrews 12:28–29

Ignatius said, "Reflect how God dwells in creatures: in the elements giving them existence, in the plants giving them life, in the animals conferring upon them sensation, in man bestowing understanding. So He dwells in me."

February 14

Permit the Creator to Deal Directly with the Creature

Therefore, the director of the Exercises, as a balance at equilibrium, without leaning to one side or the other, should permit the Creator to deal directly with the creature, and the creature directly with his Creator and Lord.

—*The Spiritual Exercises* 15

God deals directly with us: it's an idea central to Ignatian spirituality. It's a good rule for spiritual directors—and for spouses, parents, and friends anxious about those they love.

Are you helping someone make a decision or deal with a problem? Are you letting God do the work?

February 15

Constant Creation

As a being created by God, you are involved in a relationship with the Creator that gleams with a moment-by-moment immediacy. Creation is not some fatalistic scenario within which you rudely awaken, nor your own act of self-determination, nor an ancient act that long ago began the process of being. No, creation has the immediacy of constant present tense. An awareness of this immediacy at any moment can startle your soul and excite your heart in a rush of awe.

—George Aschenbrenner, SJ, *Stretched for Greater Glory*

Who is like you, O Lord, among the gods?
  Who is like you, majestic in holiness,
  awesome in splendor, doing wonders?
You stretched out your right hand,
  the earth swallowed them.
In your steadfast love you led the people whom you redeemed;
  you guided them by your strength to your holy abode.

—Exodus 15:11–13

How has God startled your soul in the past week?

February 16

What Love Is

Love ought to manifest itself in deeds rather than in words.

Love consists in a mutual sharing of goods, for example, the lover gives and shares with the beloved what he possesses, or something of that which he has or is able to give; and vice versa, the beloved shares with the lover. Hence, if one has knowledge, he shares it with the one who does not possess it; and so also if one has honours, or riches. Thus, one always gives to the other.

—*The Spiritual Exercises* 230–231

Love isn't an emotional state or flowery words but *action,* a particular kind of action—*sharing.* It's giving a gift, getting up with the baby at night, reaching out to a neglected friend.

Think about how your deeds are expressing love to others. Pay attention to what comes to mind.

February 17

St. Claude de la Colombière, SJ

Today is the feast of St. Claude de la Colombière, SJ (1641–1682), one of the most beloved Catholic teachers of the seventeenth century. He was a major supporter of the devotion to the Sacred Heart and a fierce opponent of the Jansenists, who emphasized human guilt and helplessness in the face of sin.

He said this to a dying nun who was depressed by awareness of her sins:

Do you know what would stir up my confidence, if I were as near to giving account to God as you are? It would be the number and the seriousness of my sins.

Here is a confidence really worthy of God. Far from allowing us to be depressed at the sight of our faults, it strengthens us in the idea of the infinite goodness of our Creator. Confidence inspired by purity of life does not give very much glory to God. Is this all that God's mercy can achieve—saving a soul that has never offended him? For sure the confidence of a notorious sinner honors God most of all. For he is so convinced of God's infinite mercy that all his sins seem no more than an atom in its presence.

Reread St. Claude's words of comfort. Imagine he is speaking to you. How can you embrace the truth of God's mercy?

February 18

Questions in Front of the Cross

At the end, I turn to Jesus Christ, hanging on his cross, and I talk with him. I ask how can it be that the Lord and Creator should have come from the infinite reaches of eternity to this death here on earth, so that he could die for our sins.

And then I reflect on myself, and ask:

What have I done for Christ?

What am I doing for Christ?

What ought I do for Christ?

And I talk with Jesus like a friend. I end with the Our Father.

—*The Spiritual Exercises* 53

What's my work for Christ—past, present, and future? These are the questions at the center of the Spiritual Exercises.

Set aside some time to reflect on these questions at the foot of the Cross.

February 19

Go in His Door

Whenever we wish to win someone over and engage him in the greater service of God our Lord, we should use the same strategy for good that the enemy employs to draw a good soul to evil. The enemy enters through the other's door and comes out his own. He enters with the other, not by opposing his ways but by praising them. He acts familiarly with the soul, suggesting good and holy thoughts that bring peace to the good soul. Then, little by little, he tries to come out his own door, always portraying some error or illusion under the appearance of something good, but which will always be evil. So, we may lead others to good by praying or agreeing with them on a certain good point, leaving aside whatever else may be wrong. Thus after gaining his confidence, we shall meet with better success. In this sense we enter his door with him, but we come out our own.

—St. Ignatius Loyola, *The Letters of St. Ignatius of Loyola*, William J. Young, SJ

Don't be narrow-minded and don't be dogmatic. Listen carefully to the other person with genuine respect. This is the Ignatian way.

Where are you trying to bring someone else around to your point of view? Are you looking for the good in the other's position?

February 20

God Has the Upper Hand

How many difficulties are present in the life of every individual, among our people, in our communities; yet as great as these may seem, God never allows us to be overwhelmed by them. In the face of those moments of discouragement we experience in life, in our efforts to evangelize or to embody our faith as parents within the family, I would like to say forcefully: always know in your heart that God is by your side; he never abandons you! Let us never lose hope! Let us never allow it to die in our hearts! The "dragon," evil, is present in our history, but it does not have the upper hand. The one with the upper hand is God, and God is our hope!

—Pope Francis, *The Church of Mercy*

But thanks be to God, who gives us the victory through our Lord Jesus Christ.

Therefore, my beloved, be steadfast, immovable, always excelling in the work of the Lord, because you know that in the Lord your labour is not in vain.

—1 Corinthians 15:57–58

Consider a difficult situation you are facing in light of the pope's words. Pray for greater confidence that God has the upper hand.

February 21

St. Robert Southwell, SJ

St. Robert Southwell, SJ (1561–1595), a clandestine missionary in post-Reformation England, was martyred on this day in 1595. When he was initially turned down for admission to the Jesuits, he wrote a passionate (and successful) appeal of the decision: "How can I but waste in anguish and agony because I find myself severed from that Society, disunited from that body wherein lies all my love, my whole heart and affection?"

He was a noted poet. Much of his poetry was directed to helping the oppressed Catholic minority in England find spiritual benefit in their suffering:

O dying souls! behold your living spring;
O dazzled eyes! behold your sun of grace;
Dull ears attend what word this Word doth bring;
Up, heavy hearts, with joy your joy embrace.
From death, from dark, from deafness, from despairs,
This life, this light, this Word, this joy repairs.

> [W]e also boast in our sufferings, knowing that suffering produces endurance, and endurance produces character, and character produces hope, and hope does not disappoint us, because God's love has been poured into our hearts . . .
>
> —Romans 5:3–5

Reflect on a time of personal suffering that ultimately strengthened you. How can this give you hope?

February 22

Use Natural Helps and Resources

St. Ignatius, writing to a fellow Jesuit:

You seem to hold that the use of natural helps or resources, and taking advantage of the favor of man, for ends that are good and acceptable to the Lord, is to bend the knee to Baal. Rather, it would seem that the man who thinks that it is not good to make use of such helps or to employ this talent along with others has not learned well to order all things to God's glory.

—St. Ignatius Loyola, *The Letters of St. Ignatius of Loyola*, William J. Young, SJ

Ignatius's faith was a practical faith. He embraced "natural helps and resources"; he believed that God created "the things on the face of the earth" for our good and that we are obliged to use them to help us serve God and others.

Reflect on how you have used "natural helps" to deepen your spiritual life and enhance your service to others? Can you do more of this?

February 23

Infinite Gifts

This is to consider all blessings and gifts as descending from above. Thus, my limited power comes from the supreme and infinite power above, and so, too, justice, goodness, mercy, descend from above as the rays of light descend from the sun, and as the waters flow from their fountains.

—*The Spiritual Exercises* 237

The Spiritual Exercises end with this powerful image of God as infinite gift giver. It's the picture of God that we carry into our homes, offices, and communities. It's the God we look for.

Meditate on the image of God as gift giver in the places where you will be today.

February 24

Our Jesus

Imaginative prayer makes the Jesus of the Gospels our *Jesus. It helps us develop a unique and personal relationship with him. We watch Jesus' face. We listen to the way he speaks. We notice how people respond to him. These imaginative details bring us to know Jesus as more than a name or a historical figure in a book. He is a living person. We say what the villagers in John's Gospel told the Samaritan women: "We have come to know him ourselves, and not just from your report."*

—David L. Fleming, SJ, *What Is Ignatian Spirituality?*

The Gospels are reports—accounts of Jesus' life by other people. Imaginative prayer makes them gateways into personal encounters with Jesus himself.

Spend some time imaginatively experiencing a scene from the Gospels. Scenes suggested in the Spiritual Exercises include the baptism of Jesus, the Sermon on the Mount, and the healing of Lazarus.

February 25

Questions to Ask Yourself at the End of the Day

Where in the last twenty-four hours did you experience God's touch in the events of the day?

What various energies dominated your mind and heart today? For instance,

> *experiences of satisfaction and dissatisfaction at home or at work*
>
> *experiences of interpersonal relationships with others, whether of love or rejection, that caused joy or frustration in your life*

Where have I been inattentive to the sense of beauty, truth, and goodness in my life today?

Where have I failed to respond to the needs of others?

Where do I experience regret about this day?

For what am I most grateful to God for this day?

—Jim Blumeyer, SJ, "Finding God the Ignatian Way"

This is a version of the daily examen, a method of daily prayer that Ignatius considered essential.

Take one of these questions—or two of them—and make them the focus of your reflection at the end of the day.

February 26

Concentrated Attention

Something in our soul has a far more violent repugnance for true attention than the flesh has for bodily fatigue. This something is much more closely connected with evil than is the flesh. That is why every time that we really concentrate our attention, we destroy the evil in ourselves. If we concentrate with this attention, a quarter of an hour of attention is better than a great many good works.

—Simone Weil, *Waiting for God*

The daily examen is a method for concentrating our attention on where the Lord is at work. Ignatius valued it more highly than any other prayer.

Lord, open my eyes, expand my heart, sharpen my senses—so that I can see you more clearly.

February 27

You Shouldn't Be Surprised

You speak of the enmities, the intrigues, the untruths which have been circulated about you. I am not at all surprised at this, not even if it were worse than it is. For just as soon as you determined to bend every effort to secure the praise, honor and service of God our Lord, you declared war against the world, and raised your standard in its face.

If we wish absolutely to live in honor and to be held in esteem by our neighbors, we can never be solidly rooted in God our Lord.

—St. Ignatius Loyola, *The Letters of St. Ignatius of Loyola*,
William J. Young, SJ

Blessed are you when people revile you and persecute you and utter all kinds of evil against you falsely on my account. Rejoice and be glad, for your reward is great in heaven, for in the same way they persecuted the prophets who were before you.

—Matthew 5:11–12

What is your reaction to Ignatius's comments—that misunderstanding and criticism (or worse) is the price of trying to serve the Lord? Have you experienced this?

February 28

You Can Trust Your Experience

Knowing that we can trust our experience is the first, and perhaps the most fundamental, lesson about discernment. Books and ideas and the counsel of the wise are all well and good, but the main arena for discernment is what we ourselves experience. We can discern the right direction by thoughtful reflection on our relationships with others, our work in the world, and on the feelings those encounters generated. They are meaningful because God is in them.

—J. Michael Sparough, SJ, *What's Your Decision?*

And this is my prayer, that your love may overflow more and more with knowledge and full insight to help you to determine what is best.

—Philippians 1:9–10

Consider your approach to making decisions. How have you experienced God leading you?

March 1

God Is There All the Time

Becoming aware that we have been divinized by Jesus Christ, invited into the Trinity family, is felt realization of the numinous presence of God not only all around us but also within us. God is there all the time, waiting, Atman. But, like God's forgiveness, God's will to share the divine aliveness with us can't activate until we invite it. It is the heart-stopping understanding that despite our shortcomings, despite our seeming insignificance to most of those around us, the God who dwells in unapproachable light dwells within us.

—William O'Malley, SJ, *God: The Oldest Question*

God is there all the time—not just when we are behaving well and feeling good.

Decide now how you will recall that God is with you when you are bored or anxious or weary.

March 2

The Devil Disguised as an Angel of Light

It is a mark of the evil spirit to assume the appearance of an angel of light. He begins by suggesting thoughts that are suited to a devout soul, and ends by suggesting his own. For example, he will suggest holy and pious thoughts that are wholly in conformity with the sanctity of the soul. Afterwards, he will endeavor little by little to end by drawing the soul into his hidden snares and evil designs.

—*The Spiritual Exercises* 332

Here in a nutshell is why we need discernment: poor choices and flawed plans will come to us as sensible and attractive possibilities. Ignatius's rules for discernment help us sort out the sound from the unsound, the reliable from the deceptive.

Apply this principle to any changes you are considering. Is a flawed plan cloaked in an attractive garb?

March 3

Overturning Personal Rocks

Understanding personal attachments means overturning personal rocks to see what crawls out. Attachment to money is usually salve for some other debilitating ego-itch: I'm terrified of failing; I need to feel important and be the center of attention; I'm insecure about my real talent and worth.

This is what Loyola was really *after: the internal fears, drives, and attachments that can control decisions and actions.*

—Chris Lowney, *Heroic Leadership*

The hardest work in discernment involves identifying disordered attachments—or, as Lowney puts it, overturning personal rocks.

Imagine that your fears, drives, and attachments are hidden under a rock. Turn the rock over. What walks out?

March 4

Both-And, Not Either-Or

Ignatius was always dealing with polarities: the divine and the human, the individual person and the corporate body, mission and community, spirit and law, charism and institution, the universal and the local, and so forth. The temptation when faced with such polarities, is to choose one over the other. Ignatius embraced a both-and approach. If all this brought tension, then so be it!

—Brian O'Leary, SJ, "Searching for Meaning Today: An Ignatian Contribution"

Ignatius combined this nuanced, "both-and" perspective with an ambition to achieve great things.

What are the polarities in your life? How are you living with the tension? Speak to the Lord about it.

March 5

Carry Difficulties with Strength

To suffer is to take the difficulty and to carry it with strength, so that the difficulty does not drag us down. To carry it with strength: this is a Christian virtue. Saint Paul says several times: endure. This means do not let ourselves be overcome by difficulties. This means that the Christian has the strength not to give up. Carry them, but carry them with strength. It is not easy, because discouragement comes, and one has the urge to give up and say, "Well, come on, we'll do what we can but no more." But no, it is a grace to suffer. We find so many Christians who are sad, discouraged, because they did not have this grace of enduring with patience and overcoming with love.

—Pope Francis, Vatican Radio

We ourselves boast of you among the churches of God for your steadfastness and faith during all your persecutions and the afflictions that you are enduring.

This is evidence of the righteous judgment of God, and is intended to make you worthy of the kingdom of God, for which you are also suffering.

—2 Thessalonians 1:4–5

Bring to mind a period of suffering in your life when you experienced strength to carry the burden. Thank God for that grace.

March 6

Why God Makes Us Wait

Suppose you are going to fill some holder or container, and you know you will be given a large amount. Then you set about stretching your sack or wineskin or whatever it is. Why? Because you know the quantity you will have to put in it, and your eyes tell you there is not enough room. By stretching it, therefore, you increase the capacity of the sack, and this is how God deals with us. Simply by making us wait, God increases our desire, which in turn enlarges the capacity of our soul, making it able to receive what is to be given to us.

—St. Augustine, *Homilies on the First Epistle of John*

If we hope for what we do not see, we wait for it with patience.

—Romans 8:25

Thank you, Lord, for the many blessings in my life, especially for the blessing of your love. I pray that my desire for you may grow.

March 7

Do I Really, Really Mean It?

Authenticity is the first test of my values and purpose. If I say I'm here on earth to repair the world or to be holy, do I really, really mean it? Do these ideas make me live and work differently, or do they ultimately hold no more significance than an empty slogan emblazoned across a glossy corporate annual report? Can I say that I'm here on earth for a reason, or am I simply drifting along, grasping after whatever suits a short-term need or a current fad?

—Chris Lowney, *Heroic Living*

Better the poor walking in integrity
than one perverse of speech who is a fool.

—Proverbs 19:1

What comes to mind when you reflect on the question: Does what I believe affect the way I act?

March 8

Our Lives Matter

Ignatian spirituality is rooted in the conviction that God is active, personal, and—above all—present to us. This perspective influences how we live and how we pray. The daily grind of our everyday lives takes on transcendent importance. It's the place where we connect with God. This means that the choices we make in our daily lives either push us away from God or draw us more closely to him. Our lives matter.

—IgnatianSpirituality.com

I will not leave you orphaned; I am coming to you. In a little while the world will no longer see me, but you will see me; because I live, you also will live.

—John 14:18–19

What choices can you make today that will draw you closer to God?

March 9

Listening

The first moment of Christian prayer is listening. There is a fatal instinct in all of us to reduce the word of God to the words of men. There is the tendency to confuse our own dreaming and fancies with that listening which comes from the Spirit. This kind of listening is not always easy. It has little fiction, but much hope; little sentiment, but much love; little that is flattering, but much that is fulfilling.

—John R. Sheets, SJ, *To Believe Is to Exist*

Listen—prayer isn't just about talking to God.

Bring to mind blessings or challenges you experienced yesterday. Listen to what God says about them.

March 10

The Cross Gives Meaning to Suffering

Simone Weil remarked that the extraordinary greatness of Christianity is not that it provides us with medicine against suffering, but that it gives perspective to suffering. Christianity does not spare us pain. The Gospel does not promise that we will not suffer. Indeed, the Gospel makes it very clear that we do have to lose our lives, to take up our cross and follow Christ. And that is unique! All other religions either try to avoid pain or make one immune to it so that it will no longer be felt. This is not the Gospel approach.

—Peter van Breemen, SJ, *As Bread That Is Broken*

May I never boast of anything except the cross of our Lord Jesus Christ.

—Galatians 6:14

Reflect on the quote by van Breemen. Allow God to deepen your understanding of suffering.

March 11

Human Ingenuity or the Hand of God?

How are we to interpret the alternately serendipitous and disappointing, unexpected and unpredictable, courses of our lives? What is happening when death or financial disaster forces us to reconsider what we want from life, when teachers or mentors find and nurture talent we didn't know we had, when we succeed beyond our wildest imaginings, when managers steer our careers in fortuitous directions, when we aren't offered the job we wanted so badly? Do such cases merely vindicate human ingenuity, resilience, fortitude, and imagination? Or is God, too, at work in some ineffable way?

Well, why not both? That's how I read Ignatius, the former military commander and take-charge, type-A personality who nonetheless attuned himself to read God's will in the subtle promptings of consolations and desolations. Or, as expressed in a great mantra of Jesuit spirituality, "Find God in all things."

—Chris Lowney, *Heroic Living*

We speak God's wisdom, secret and hidden, which God decreed before the ages for our glory.

—1 Corinthians 2:7

In what situations do you need to find a more balanced view of how God works in your life?

March 12

Real Religion

The maxim of illusory religion runs: "Fear not; trust in God and He will see that none of the things you fear will happen to you"; that of real religion, on the contrary, is "Fear not; the things that you are afraid of are quite likely to happen to you, but they are nothing to be afraid of."

—John Macmurray, *Persons in Relation*

Do not fear, for I am with you,
  do not be afraid, for I am your God;
I will strengthen you, I will help you,
  I will uphold you with my victorious right hand.

—Isaiah 41:10

Pray the psalm verses above. Take those words into your heart.

March 13

I Must Surrender Myself Completely

One thing is becoming gradually clear—I must surrender myself completely. This is seedtime, not harvest. God sows the seed and some time or other he will do the reaping. The one thing I must do is to make sure the seed falls on fertile ground. And I must arm myself against the pain and depression that sometimes almost defeat me. If this is the way God has chosen—and everything indicates that it is—then I must willingly and without rancor make it my way.

—Alfred Delp, SJ, *With Bound Hands*

And going a little farther, he threw himself on the ground and prayed that, if it were possible, the hour might pass from him. He said, "Abba, Father, for you all things are possible; remove this cup from me; yet, not what I want, but what you want."

—Mark 14:35–36

Delp writes, "I must surrender myself completely." Where do you need to surrender?

March 14

You Are Not Alone

When we are feeling lonely—if we are brave enough to resist the urge to call someone up, or go shopping, or take a drug, or turn to music or TV or go to bed; if we are courageous enough to remain alone and instead of fleeing the pain, to go down into it—we will gradually notice another Presence there, silent, but benevolent and peaceful.

—Karl Rahner, SJ, in *Spiritual Quest*, Thomas Hart

From there you will seek the LORD your God, and you will find him if you search after him with all your heart and soul.

—Deuteronomy 4:29

Create a still, silent space today. Shut off the music; turn off the phone. Notice the Presence.

March 15

Do It Now!

When he heard anyone saying, "I will do this two weeks from now, or a week from now," Father Ignatius was always a bit amazed: "How's that? Do you count on living that long?"

—Luis Gonçalves da Camara, SJ, in *A Pilgrim's Journey*, Joseph N. Tylenda, SJ

Come now, you who say, "Today or tomorrow we will go to such and such a town and spend a year there, doing business and making money." Yet you do not even know what tomorrow will bring. What is your life? For you are a mist that appears for a little while and then vanishes.

—James 4:13–14

What task are you putting off that you can do today?

March 16

Christ on a Mission

The Ignatian view of Christ is that of Christ on mission—preaching, teaching, healing. The decision to follow Christ is to follow him as humble, poor, and rejected within a culture that values wealth, power, influence, and prestige. The virtues Ignatius emphasizes are those of freedom, magnanimity, and self-sacrifice, which lead to doing great deeds in the world for the sake of the gospel. The Exercises are relentlessly oriented toward the life one lives outside of solitude—in the arena of public life, to the future.

—Howard Gray, SJ, *The Experience of Ignatius Loyola: Background to Jesuit Education*

Freedom, magnanimity, and self-sacrifice—active virtues for an active life of service.

What is Christ calling you to do today? What do you need from God to do the work?

March 17

Pray for Our Enemies

Too often we become enemies of others: we do not wish them well. And Jesus tells us to love our enemies! And this is not easy! Let me just ask this question and let each of us answer it in our own heart: "Do I pray for my enemies? Do I pray for those who do not love me?" If we say "yes," I will say, "Go on, pray more, you are on the right path!"

—Pope Francis, Vatican Radio

> Do not repay anyone evil for evil, but take thought for what is noble in the sight of all. If it is possible, so far as it depends on you, live peaceably with all.
>
> —Romans 12:17–18

Consider those who cause you distress, who thwart your plans. Ask the pope's question: Do I pray for them?

March 18

The Present Moment Is the Only Real Moment

The spiritual life always concerns itself with the present. Retreatants are very inclined to worry about the future and be guilty about the past. It is important to set goals for the future and to implement ways to achieve those goals. It is also important to review the past, claim the history of grace and sin and more grace. But the Present Moment is the only real moment. Directors of the Exercises are always inviting retreatants to live in the now moment, because the present is the only moment of grace.

—Bill Creed, SJ, unpublished manuscript

Say goodbye
to golden yesterdays
—or your heart
will never learn
to love
the present.

—Anthony de Mello, SJ, *Wellsprings*

Pause in your activities today—perhaps when you are in the car, or between meetings—and be still in the present moment of grace.

March 19

God Is Now

With God we always start exactly where we are. I can now see several places where I took the wrong turn. In Ignatius's language, I made the wrong "election." So what can I do about it now? Stand and regret? Or go back to the bottom of the hill and try again? Or remember that God is Now and God is Here, wherever we are, in whatever unchosen places or situations, and that it is God whom we seek, not a particular path.

—Lisa Kelly, *This Ignatian Life* blog

Note the simplicity of it: If we seek God first, we have the confidence to weather any storm and overcome any disappointment. God is here. Now. We can begin again.

Recalling that God is here, now, what regret can you begin to let go of?

March 20

The Problem with Being Hard on Yourself

Ignatius, writing to another Jesuit:

There are two drawbacks in dealing with yourself so severely. The first is that without a miracle your reverence will not last long in the holy ministries, which would be to put quite an obstacle in the way of God's service and the help of souls. The second is that, being so harsh with yourself, you could easily come to be excessively so with those under your charge. And even though you give them no more than your example, it must result in making some of them run too fast.

—St. Ignatius Loyola, *The Letters of St. Ignatius of Loyola*, William J. Young, SJ

Ignatius's second point is an observation about the nature of personal leadership. A leader's "personal preferences" are often public; they're noticed and imitated.

Reflect on the example you are giving to family, friends, and others who are personally connected to you.

March 21

Deeper Than Mere Compassion

The poor, the suffering, the disadvantaged, must stand at the very center of our concern. For they need justice as much as anyone else; only they can neither buy it nor impose it. It was left for God to bring the good news to the poor. But God is not only the God of *the poor. God is God who* is *poor. For the mystery of the Incarnation has established a special relationship between God and poverty whose meaning goes much deeper than mere compassion.*

—Pedro Arrupe, SJ, in *The Ignatian Tradition*, Kevin F. Burke, Eileen Burke-Sullivan, Phyllis Zagano

This is a most challenging idea—God's connection to the poor and suffering is so deep that a response of compassion is insufficient. What might this response be?

Who is poor in your circle? How can your response go beyond compassion?

March 22

Luis Espinal, SJ

Luis Espinal, SJ, a Spanish Jesuit who worked for social justice in Bolivia, was murdered on this day in 1980. He wrote:

Losing one's life means working for others, even though they don't pay us back. It means doing a favor without it being returned. Losing one's life means jumping in even when failure is the likely outcome—and doing it without being overly prudent. It means burning bridges for the sake of our neighbor.

Losing one's life should not be accompanied by pompous or dramatic gestures. Life is to be given simply, without fanfare—like a waterfall, like a mother nursing her child, like the humble sweat of the sower of seed.

—In *Base Communites*, Margaret Hebblethwaite

Do nothing from selfish ambition or conceit, but in humility regard others as better than yourselves. Let each of you look not to your own interests, but to the interests of others.

—Philippians 2:3–4

Consider someone you know who serves others with generosity and humility. Reflect on how their service reveals God to you.

March 23

Prayer at the Deepest Level

We pray then at our deepest level because we are drawn by the bonds of love. We pray because we love, and not just for utilitarian purposes. If prayer has beneficial effects, that is because prayer corresponds to our deepest reality. When we are in tune with God, we cannot help but experience deep well-being. Ignatius of Loyola spoke of consolation as a sign of a person's being in tune with God's intention. But in the final analysis, the lover does not spend time with the Beloved because of the consolation; the lover just wants to be with the Beloved.

—William Barry, SJ, *God's Passionate Desire*

I bless the LORD who gives me counsel;
  in the night also my heart instructs me.
I keep the LORD always before me;
  because he is at my right hand, I shall not be moved.

—Psalm 16:7–8

Recall a time when you have experienced deep communion with God. Give thanks for this.

March 24

A Conversation with God

Jesus' way *of praying is more important than the words he taught us. We are personally familiar with God (*"our *Father"). We reverence him ("hallowed be thy name"). We share God's desires ("thy kingdom come," "thy will be done"). We ask for what we need ("give us this day our daily bread"). We beg our Father's protection ("deliver us from evil").*

These elements of prayer cover the whole range of human conversation: sharing experience, saying thank you, asking for help, crying out in pain, begging forgiveness, expressing love, just spending time together. This is what we do when we get together with our friends.

—David L. Fleming, SJ, *What Is Ignatian Spirituality?*

I do not call you servants any longer, because the servant does not know what the master is doing; but I have called you friends, because I have made known to you everything that I have heard from my Father. You did not choose me but I chose you.

—John 15:15–16

In prayer today, spend some time speaking to Christ as a friend. As Ignatius puts it, "as one friend to another . . . making known his affairs to him, and seeking advice in them."

March 25

Ignatius Arrives at Manresa

On this day in 1522, Ignatius arrived at the village Manresa on the Cardoner River in northern Spain. The eleven months he spent at Manresa were crucial to the development of his spirituality and to his understanding of his life's work. He began to compile the reflections about his spiritual life that developed into the *Spiritual Exercises*. He adopted and then abandoned severe spiritual practices, begged for food, took care of poor people, and spent many hours in prayer. He had mystical visions. He described the most important one this way:

He sat down for a little while with his face to the river—Cardoner—which was running deep. While he was seated there, the eyes of his understanding began to be opened; though he did not see any vision, he understood and knew many things, both spiritual things and matters of faith and learning, and this was with so great an enlightenment that everything seemed new to him. It was as if he were a new man with a new intellect.

—In *A Pilgrim's Journey*, Joseph N. Tylenda, SJ

Recall a time when the eyes of your understanding were gradually opened. How did this affect your life?

March 26

Ignatius's Management Style

One of Ignatius's secretaries, Luis Gonçalves da Camara, describes his management style and method of making decisions.

Father Ignatius is accustomed to being so firm in things which he undertakes, that this steadfastness amazes everyone. Here are the reasons that come to my mind. First is that he carefully considers each matter before deciding it. Second, he prays very much on this subject and is illuminated by God. Third, he makes no particular decision without hearing the opinion of those who are competent in the matter.

—Luis Gonçalves da Camara, SJ, in *Ignatius of Loyola: The Psychology of a Saint*, William Meissner, SJ

A fool takes no pleasure in understanding,
but only in expressing personal opinion.
If one gives answer before hearing,
it is folly and shame.

—Proverbs 18:2,13

Review Ignatius's habits of decision making. What can you learn from them?

March 27

We Are Not in Control

Only God can save us from our fears and our addictions. Many of us need to hit a wall in order to have a chance of waking up to the reality that we are living insane lives as long as we believe that we can control things on our own. When we wake up to the real world, we find God patiently waiting for us, ready to help, ready to save us and make us whole.

—William Barry, SJ, "The First Commandment and Sanity," *Human Development*

Giving up control can be very difficult. The task is made easier when we recognize that the notion that we control things is largely an illusion.

Where do you try to control events and other people? Talk to God about relinquishing this impulse.

March 28

Experience God from the Inside Out

Many religions provide a long list of things to be wary of, shunned, despised. Ignatian spirituality offers an alternative means to discerning what is "of God." Rather than provide for people definitive lists of what is "in" and what is "out," Ignatius implored retreatants to seek the experience of God from the inside out, constantly discerning awareness of any "disordered inclinations" that are leading us away from God as well as those things that gave us peace and a sense of consolation. He noted that often those things that we most fear, most get stirred up over, or consider a weakness are instead the Spirit Not of God preventing us from being open to where God is calling.

—Lisa Kelly, *This Ignatian Life* blog

Here's one of the better descriptions of what's distinctive about Ignatian spirituality. It takes seriously the conflict in our divided hearts instead of claiming that the righteous can be free from troubles.

Ponder this: What you fear may well point to where God is working in you.

March 29

Salvation Is Not Comfortable

Salvation is not comfortable. There is something terrifying about it. Salvation is not a gentle application of Vaseline to a small cut, but the breaking and resetting of ill-set bones. We discover our need when we are faced with situations over which we have no control, and in which we have no hope. When the sick know that their "sickness is unto death" and they cannot save themselves, then they hear the voice telling them "take up your bed and walk"—for salvation is at hand.

—John Harriott, SJ, "Ourselves We Cannot Save"

Work out your own salvation with fear and trembling; for it is God who is at work in you, enabling you both to will and to work for his good pleasure.

—Philippians 2:12–13

Reflect on this idea—that there's something frightening about salvation.

March 30

Karl Rahner, SJ

Karl Rahner, SJ, one of the most influential theologians of the twentieth century, died on this day in 1984. Rahner believed that academic theology was not an end in itself but should serve the life and mission of the Church. He was a spiritual director, retreat leader, and spiritual writer who worked tirelessly to find food, shelter, and clothing for those in need.

He addressed these words to Jesuits, but they apply to all persons of faith:

Our faith must be such that even the unbeliever cannot deny that here a man believes who is like himself, a man of today, on whose lips the word God does not come easily and cheaply, who doesn't think he has mastered everything, and in spite of all this, rather because of all this, he believes.

For Christianity is not a formula which makes everything clear, but the radical submission of myself to an incomprehensible Mystery Who has revealed Himself as ineffable love.

—"The Faith of the Priest Today," *The Woodstock Letters: A Record*

What would an unbeliever see in you that would identify you as a person of faith?

March 31

The Purpose of the Society of Jesus

The Society is founded chiefly for this purpose: to strive especially for the defense and propagation of the faith and for the progress of souls in Christian life and doctrine, by means of public preaching, lectures and any other ministration whatsoever of the word of God, and further by means of the Spiritual Exercises, the education of children and unlettered persons in Christianity, and the spiritual consolation of Christ's faithful through hearing confessions and administering the sacraments.

—*Constitutions of the Society of Jesus*

Ignatius put it more concisely in his Autobiography, where he wrote that the Jesuits "would pass their whole lives in helping souls."

In what ways do you participate in the Jesuits' purpose?

April 1

God Can Be Found in All Things

"All things" to Ignatius is the whole panoply of the human drama—our relationships, our work, our strivings and failures, our hopes and dreams. God can be found in all of it. Found *does not mean an intellectual exercise of perceiving the presence of the divine. It means engaging God in it, meeting him, dealing with him. It is a matter of* conversar*—an intimate conversation and the interacting that takes place between family members who love each other.*

—David L. Fleming, SJ, *What Is Ignatian Spirituality?*

Finding God in all things is personal, a matter of the heart more than the mind—opening the eyes of the heart to see God in all things, filling the heart with zeal to follow Christ wherever he leads.

In the last twenty-four hours, where has your heart sensed the presence of God?

April 2

Humility and Hope

He who enjoys consolation should take care to humble himself and lower himself as much as possible. Let him recall how little he is able to do in time of desolation, when he is left without such grace or consolation.

On the other hand, one who suffers desolation should remember that by making use of the sufficient grace offered him, he can do much to withstand all his enemies. Let him find strength in his Creator and Lord.

—*The Spiritual Exercises* 324

The happy should be humble; the suffering should be hopeful. Humility and hope—two themes that resonate throughout Ignatius's teaching. All we have comes from God, and God gives us all that we need.

Where do you need more humility or more hope right now?

April 3

Pray as If Everything Depends on You

There's an old saying that we should "pray as if everything depends on God, work as if everything depends on you." It's been attributed to Ignatius (though there's no evidence that he said it), and many think it captures the Ignatian spirit: turning it all over to God in prayer and then working tirelessly to do God's work. I prefer to reverse it: "pray as if everything depends on you, work as if everything depends on God." This means that prayer has to be urgent: God has to do something dramatic if everything depends on me. It also puts our work in the right perspective: if it depends on God, we can let it go. We can work hard but leave the outcome up to him.

—Jim Manney, *Dot Magis* blog

Ignatius wrote to a friend, "There is no need to wear yourself out, but make a competent and sufficient effort, and leave the rest to him."

Would you rather pray as if everything depends on God or as if everything depends on you? Why?

April 4

Fully Present

Ignatian spirituality is about the exact opposite of letting your mind wander carelessly in prayer. It is about being fully present to the moment, every moment, including those during prayer and those throughout the day. The depth of Ignatian prayer comes not from saying any particular words or incantation, but from being fully in a moment of relationship with Christ.

—Margaret Silf, *Inner Compass*

I bless the Lord who gives me counsel;
  in the night also my heart instructs me.
I keep the Lord always before me;
  because he is at my right hand, I shall not be moved.

Therefore my heart is glad, and my soul rejoices;
  my body also rests secure.
For you do not give me up to Sheol,
  or let your faithful one see the Pit.

You show me the path of life.
  In your presence there is fullness of joy;
  in your right hand are pleasures for evermore.

—Psalm 16:7–11

Resolved: I will strive to be fully present to Christ in prayer today—and fully present to the people I'm with today.

April 5

The Most Abominable of Sins

It seems to me in the light of the Divine Goodness, although others may think differently, that ingratitude is the most abominable of sins and that it should be detested in the sight of our Creator and Lord by all of His creatures. For it is a forgetting of the graces, benefits, and blessings received. As such it is the cause, beginning, and origin of all sins and misfortunes. On the contrary, the grateful acknowledgment of blessings and gifts received is loved and esteemed not only on earth but in heaven.

—St. Ignatius Loyola, *The Letters of St. Ignatius of Loyola*,
William J. Young, SJ

If ingratitude is the root of all sin, then gratitude is the queen of virtues.

Spend some time today making a gratitude list—a list of the blessings you have received from God.

April 6

Surprise Me

One of my favorite novels is *Mariette in Ecstasy* by Ron Hansen, a story about a young nun who has mystical visions. The novel ends with these words, from a letter Mariette writes to a friend long after she has left the community:

And Christ still sends me roses. We try to be formed and held and kept by him, but instead he offers us freedom. And now when I try to know his will, his kindness floods me, his great love overwhelms me, and I hear him whisper, Surprise me.

Can we surprise God? Probably not in some ultimate metaphysical sense; God knows all in his dwelling place in eternity. But in our daily relationship with Jesus—I wouldn't dismiss the idea out of hand. We crave certainty; "instead he offers us freedom." This opens the door to surprise. Even if we don't surprise God, we can surprise ourselves.

> I am about to do a new thing;
> now it springs forth, do you not perceive it?
>
> —Isaiah 43:19

Make me free, Lord. Open my heart for surprises.

April 7

We Are Never Alone

We are one body; we are one in Jesus. He is our brother and he identifies with us, completely. None of us can ever say we are alone. And, as members of this body, we can ask for the grace to grow in a sense of feeling, sensing, appreciating that when any one of us suffers, the whole of us suffer—because we are connected.

Of course, this is difficult to experience while we feel alienated, angry, threatened by one of our brothers or sisters. But, it all becomes possible and makes sense, when we let ourselves experience conversion, and receive a new mission, a new purpose.

—Andy Alexander, SJ, Creighton University's Online Ministries

For just as the body is one and has many members, and all the members of the body, though many, are one body, so it is with Christ. For in the one Spirit we were all baptized into one body—Jews or Greeks, slaves or free—and we were all made to drink of one Spirit.

—1 Corinthians 12:12–13

Pray for the grace to experience conversion and change in relationships that are blocked and difficult.

April 8

What the Poor Teach Us

The poor are the privileged teachers of our knowledge of God; their frailty and simplicity unmask our selfishness, our false security, and our claim to be self-sufficient. The poor guide us to experience God's closeness and tenderness, to receive his love in our life, his mercy as the Father who cares for us, for all of us, with discretion and patient trust. From this place of welcome, encounter, and service, I would therefore like to launch a question to everyone . . . Do I bend down over someone in difficulty, or am I afraid of getting my hands dirty? Am I closed in on myself and my possessions, or am I aware of those in need of help? Do I serve only myself, or am I able to serve others, like Christ who came to serve even to the point of giving up his life?

—Pope Francis, *The Church of Mercy*

And the king will answer them, "Truly I tell you, just as you did it to one of the least of these who are members of my family, you did it to me."

—Matthew 25:40

How do you "bend down" over people in difficulty? Do you have personal contact with those in need?

April 9

The Trouble with Keeping Secrets

When the enemy of our human nature tempts a just soul with his wiles and seductions, he earnestly desires that they be received secretly and kept secret. But if one manifests them to a confessor, or to some other spiritual person who understands his deceits and malicious designs, the evil one is very much vexed. For he knows that he cannot succeed in his evil undertaking, once his evident deceits have been revealed.

—*The Spiritual Exercises* 236

"I don't want to talk about it." "Let's move on." "It's nothing." When you're inclined to keep things to yourself, beware.

Are you inclined to stay silent about something that distresses you?
Who can you share troubles with?

April 10

Pierre Teilhard de Chardin, SJ

Pierre Teilhard de Chardin, SJ, a French paleontologist, theologian, and mystic, died on this day in 1955 in New York City. Chardin was trained as a scientist, and he made significant contributions to the study of the origins of the human race. His theological interests increasingly turned to the relationship between the evolution of the material world and the sacredness of matter infused with the divine presence. Ecclesiastical authorities were suspicious of his ideas, and they prevented him from publishing his books for many years. These bans have since been lifted, and Chardin is now regarded as an important thinker and spiritual writer.

He wrote:

God is not altogether apart from the world we see, touch, hear, smell, and taste around us. Rather he awaits us every instant in our action, in the work of the moment. There is a sense in which he is at the tip of my pen, my spade, my brush, my needle. By pressing the stroke, the line, or the stitch, on which I am engaged, to its ultimate natural finish, I shall lay hold of that last end toward which my innermost will tends.

—*The Divine Milieu*

Listen! I am standing at the door, knocking; if you hear my voice and open the door, I will come in to you and eat with you, and you with me.

—Revelation 3:20

Imagine the Lord waiting for you as you approach each task in the day ahead.

April 11

What I Want and Desire

This is to ask for what I desire. Here it will be to ask for an intimate knowledge of the many blessings received, that filled with gratitude for all, I may in all things love and serve the Divine Majesty.

—*The Spiritual Exercises* 233

Note that the knowledge of gifts is to be "intimate"—personal, close, the fruit of a relationship. Also, gratitude motivates us to love and serve God. That puts gratitude at the top of the list of virtues.

Pray for an intimate knowledge of the many blessings you have received.

April 12

Don't Try to Live Someone Else's Life

Ultimately our deepest desires are those that God has planted within us. So the notion of vocation (from the Latin word vocare, *meaning "to call") is less about finding one and more about having it revealed to us. As Thomas Merton wrote, "For me to be a saint means to be myself."*

Part of that means letting go of the wish to lead someone else's life, and remembering that our own vocations—not somebody else's—are what will finally lead us to happiness. You don't need to use anyone else's map to heaven, because God has already placed within your soul all the directions you'll ever need.

—James Martin, SJ, "Be Who You Is," *Santa Clara Magazine*

A striking notion: we don't find a vocation; it's revealed to us. God has planted our call deep within us.

How would you describe your vocation in this Ignatian sense—a call discerned through desires that God has given you?

April 13

The Red-Letter Day in Your Spiritual Life

When I was a novice, our novice master would say to us, "the red letter day in your spiritual life will come, not when you believe that you love God, but when you realize that he *loves* you*!" Many years of experience (experience of others and my own) have shown me how right he was. What a transformation occurs in our lives, how rapidly we begin to change, when we realize how much and how unconditionally he loves and accepts us.*

—Anthony de Mello, SJ, *Contact with God*

O give thanks to the Lord, for he is good;
for his steadfast love endures for ever.

—Psalm 107:1

Spend a few minutes giving thanks to God for his unconditional love for you.

April 14

Three Consequences of Doing Things to Excess

The first is that God is not really served in the long run, as the horse worn out in the first days does not, as a rule, finish the journey.

Second, gains that are made with this excessive eagerness are not usually kept. "One who moves too hurriedly misses the way" (Proverbs 19:2); and if he missteps, the further he falls, for he will not stop until he has reached the bottom of the ladder.

Third, there is the danger of being careless about overloading the vessel. There is danger, of course, in sailing it empty, as it can then be tossed about on the waves of temptation. But there is also danger of so overloading it as to cause it to sink.

—St. Ignatius Loyola, *The Letters of St. Ignatius of Loyola*, William J. Young, SJ

A horse, a ladder, a ship—these are metaphors from a wise teacher counseling balance and moderation.

Talk to God about the balance in your life. Is the ship empty or overloaded?

April 15

The Most Perfect Kind of Humility

This is the most perfect kind of humility. It consists in this. . . . whenever the praise and glory of the Divine Majesty would be equally served, in order to imitate and be in reality more like Christ our Lord, I desire and choose poverty with Christ poor, rather than riches; insults with Christ loaded with them, rather than honors; I desire to be accounted as worthless and a fool for Christ, rather than to be esteemed as wise and prudent in this world. So Christ was treated before me.

—*The Spiritual Exercises* 167

This account of perfect humility is one of the "hard sayings" of the Spiritual Exercises. Is it possible to become humble in this way? Ignatius never says that anyone *should* become perfectly humble. He proposes it as something on which to ponder and reflect.

Reflect on this description of humility. Talk to the Lord about it.

April 16

Centered on Christ

There is one prayer in the Exercises which never varies in all the meditations: "I will beg God our Lord for the grace that all my intentions, actions and operations may be directed purely to the service and praise of His Divine Majesty." The Exercises are not centered on our feelings and emotions; they are centered on Christ. It is in the light of God's revelation in Christ, and in the faith that "God is in all things and all things in him" that we consider ourselves. "What have I done for him? What will I do for him?"

—Gerard Hughes, SJ, "Forgotten Truths"

Ignatian spirituality is centered on Christ. The central questions from the Spiritual Exercises are "What have I done for Christ?" "What am I doing for Christ?" "What ought I to do for Christ?"

Pray the prayer: "I will beg God our Lord for the grace that all my intentions, actions and operations may be directed purely to the service and praise of His Divine Majesty."

April 17

"Talk to Him about How He Creates because He Loves"

Early in the Exercises, Ignatius asks the retreatant to pray before Jesus Christ on the cross. "Talk to him about how he creates because he loves," Ignatius seems to say.

This is no abstract God of reason, but a loving God seen in the face of Jesus Christ. Our spiritual journey is an attempt to answer the question, "What is life all about?" Here is Ignatius's answer: a vision of God for our hearts, not our minds. It is a depiction of the Creator as a superabundant giver. He gives gifts that call forth a response on our part, a free choice to return ourselves to him in grateful thanks and love.

—David L. Fleming, SJ, *What Is Ignatian Spirituality?*

The mind asks, "What is life all about?" The heart answers with a vision of endless, abundant giving. Giving is what life is all about.

Talk to God about how he creates because he loves.

April 18

The Difference between Happiness and Hopelessness

We are not aimless beings, without a goal or purpose. We have been created by a God Who loves us. We are called to build the Kingdom of God by knowing, loving and serving God and other people and thus entering life everlasting. The values, priorities and fundamental commitments that really steer us at the level of our heart as well as our minds flow from such a purpose; they make all the difference between happiness and hopelessness.

—Peter-Hans Kolvenbach, SJ, "Message to Friends and Colleagues of the Society of Jesus"

The difference lies in our hearts more than our minds: "What am I passionate about?" more than "What am I convinced of?"

What are you passionate about?

April 19

A Litany of Gratitude

Begin by picturing yourself in God's presence, ask God to give you awareness of all the gifts God has given you over the course of your life, and ask further for a spirit of gratitude. As you pay attention to these gifts, consider the ways that you might use them for God's greater glory and how you might offer them back to God.

Give thanks for Creation itself.
Your ancestors and those who struggled to give you life,
Your biological mother and father, whether you know them or not,
Your immediate family, whether related by blood or not,
Your body, whether you like the way it is or not,
Your faculties of sense, even if some seem faulty,
Your intelligence, whether or not you think you have enough of it,
Your special talents, whether or not you think them useful,
Your friends and loved ones, whether alive or dead,
Your work, whether for money or not,
Your play, even though it may seem infrequent,
Your possessions, no matter how much money they are worth,
Your time to live, no matter how quickly it seems to pass.

—Tim Muldoon, *The Ignatian Workout*

Do everything in the name of the Lord Jesus, giving thanks to God the Father through him.

—Colossians 3:17

Pray the litany every day for the next several days.

April 20

Little Things with Great Love

The quality with which a work is done can be more important than the sheer quantity of tasks a person completes. What value, for example, that a social worker counsels fifty people a day if each feels like a processed can rolling through an assembly line? Or what value is there in people parroting hundreds of prayers without real conscious engagement? As Archbishop Oscar Romero said: "We cannot do everything and there is a sense of liberation in realizing that. This enables us to do something and do it very well." Or as Mother Teresa put it: "We cannot do great things on this earth; we can only do little things with great love."

—Chris Lowney, *Heroic Living*

This is the Ignatian *magis*—perpetual striving to do small things as well as we possibly can.

Ask the Lord to bring to mind a small task that you can do better and with greater love.

April 21

Amazing Grace

St. Augustine was impressed by the amount of sin in the world; humanity for him was a massa damnata. *That seems to imply that grace is not only unearned but bestowed sparingly. Ignatius, on the other hand, was impressed by the fact that God spoke to him despite his sinfulness. That implied a liberality to God's giving and forgiving. If God would speak to him, he would speak to anyone.*

—Ronald Modras, *Ignatian Humanism*

You did not choose me but I chose you.

—John 15:16

Spend some time today thanking God for choosing you.

April 22

The First Jesuits Profess Their Vows

On this day in 1541, the first Jesuits professed their formal vows in a ceremony at the Basilica of St. Paul Outside the Walls in Rome. Three days earlier, on April 19, Ignatius had reluctantly accepted his election to be the first superior general of the order. Ignatius and five companions made the profession together; four others were abroad.

Before the Holy Communion, Ignatius held the sacred host in one hand and the text of the vows in the other. He said his profession. Then he put five eucharistic hosts on the paten and turned to the five companions. Each single one said his profession and received the Eucharist. After the Mass they met at the altar where St. Paul's bones are kept. There they gave each other the kiss of peace "with much devotion, emotion and comfort."

> Rejoice in the Lord always; again I will say, Rejoice. Let your gentleness be known to everyone. The Lord is near. Do not worry about anything, but in everything by prayer and supplication with thanksgiving let your requests be made known to God. And the peace of God, which surpasses all understanding, will guard your hearts and your minds in Christ Jesus.
>
> —Philippians 4:4–7

Reflect on your most important commitments. Speak to the Lord about them.

April 23

Put on the Lord Jesus

For a Christian, to be holy is to put on the Lord Jesus, to live "now not with my own life but with the life of Christ who lives in me" (Gal 2:20). Christian holiness is a way of life, as it was in the Old Testament. But now this means not primarily a life of faithful observance of the law, but a life of loving intimacy with the Father, lived through, with, and in Jesus Christ.

—Thomas Green, SJ, *Prayer and Common Sense*

All who are led by the Spirit of God are children of God. For you did not receive a spirit of slavery to fall back into fear, but you have received a spirit of adoption. When we cry, "Abba! Father!" it is that very Spirit bearing witness with our spirit that we are children of God, and if children, then heirs, heirs of God and joint heirs with Christ.

—Romans 8:14–17

Ask Jesus how you can grow closer to the Father. Listen to what he says.

April 24

Teach Me to Listen

Teach me to listen, O God, to those nearest me, my family, my friends, my co-workers.

Help me to be aware that no matter what words I hear, the message is, "Accept the person I am. Listen to me."

Teach me to listen, my caring God, to those far from me—the whisper of the hopeless, the plea of the forgotten, the cry of the anguished.

Teach me to listen, O God my Mother, to myself. Help me to be less afraid to trust the voice inside—in the deepest part of me.

Teach me to listen, Holy Spirit, for your voice—in busyness and in boredom, in certainty and doubt, in noise and in silence.

Teach me, Lord, to listen. Amen.

—John Veltri, SJ, *Orientations for Spiritual Growth*

You must understand this, my beloved: let everyone be quick to listen, slow to speak, slow to anger.

—James 1:19

Pray the prayer again, slowly. What do you hear?

April 25

What to Do about Distractions

People say, "I become distracted whenever I try to pray." My response to this is to suggest that people make the distraction the content of their prayer, to hear God's word in this person, situation, whatever it might be. It is usually the very situation or person that we should be thinking, reflecting, praying about in the presence of the Lord. So I think most of the distractions we get are really not distractions.

—J.J. O'Leary, SJ, *Finding God in All Things: A Marquette Prayer Book*

Let the words of my mouth and the meditation of my heart
be acceptable to you, O Lord, my rock and my redeemer.

—Psalm 19:14

Follow Fr. O'Leary's advice; make distractions part of your prayer.

April 26

The Grace of Shame

Ask for the grace of shame; the shame that comes from the constant dialogue of mercy with Him; the shame that makes us blush before Jesus Christ; the shame that puts us in tune with the heart of Christ . . .; the shame that harmonizes our heart in tears and accompanies us in the daily following of "my Lord." And this always brings us, as individuals and as a Company, to humility, to living this great virtue. Humility that makes us understand, each day, that it is not for us to build the Kingdom of God, but it is always the grace of God working within us; humility that pushes us to put our whole being not at the service of ourselves and our own ideas, but at the service of Christ and of the Church, like clay pots, fragile, inadequate, insufficient, but having within them an immense treasure that we carry and that we communicate (2 Cor 4:7).

—Pope Francis, Vatican Radio

For we do not proclaim ourselves; we proclaim Jesus Christ as Lord and ourselves as your slaves for Jesus' sake.

—2 Corinthians 4:5

Lord, I pray for the humility that puts me in tune with your heart of mercy.

April 27

A Prayer Exercise

Reflect on a time when you were clearly in a period of consolation—that is, a time of deep inner peace, during which you experienced great desires of faith, hope, and love. Go back to that place of deep inner peace. Here are a few ways you might reflect on moments of consolation.

What is the peace of Christ like? How do you experience it? How is it not the peace that the world gives?

Ponder how close you felt to God then and how natural it seemed to move toward greater faith, greater hope, and greater love.

Remember how easy it was to recognize "God laboring through all created things and events," as St. Ignatius put it. See how clear it was for you to see God's hand in every aspect of life, even the difficult ones.

—Mark E. Thibodeaux, SJ, *God's Voice Within*

And let the peace of Christ rule in your hearts, to which indeed you were called in the one body. And be thankful. Let the word of Christ dwell in you richly.

—Colossians 3:15–16

Do the prayer exercise.

April 28

Counterfeit Humility

When he sees someone so good and humble [as you are], the devil is ready with the suggestion that, should the Lord's servant happen to speak of the graces our Lord has bestowed upon him, he sins in speaking favorably of himself. In this way he tries to prevent him from speaking of any of the blessings he has received. His purpose is to prevent him from producing fruit in others. Thus, when the enemy of our salvation sees that we are humble, he tries to draw us on to a humility that is excessive and counterfeit.

—St. Ignatius Loyola, *The Letters of St. Ignatius of Loyola*, William J. Young, SJ

Boasting isn't humility, but ignoring or minimizing one's gifts and accomplishments isn't humility either.

How do you tend to assess your abilities? Do you minimize them? Exaggerate them?

April 29

Sin Is a Message of Hope

The Ignatian approach to spirituality says that the traditional Christian doctrine of original sin is not a message of doom is but one of hope. It declares that the world as we have it is not the best we can hope for, nor the world that God intends, but a badly broken and distorted one which can be restored.

—Monika Hellwig, "Finding God in All Things: A Spirituality for Today"

O truly necessary sin of Adam,
destroyed completely by the Death of Christ!
O happy fault
that earned for us so great, so glorious a Redeemer!

—The Easter Proclamation (Exsultet)

Consider current disturbing and tragic events in the world in light of this comment—that sin is a message of hope.

April 30

The Flesh of Christ

When I used to go to hear confessions in my previous diocese, people would come to me, and I would always ask them: "Do you give alms?" "Yes, Father!" *"Very good." And I would ask them two further questions: "Tell me, when you give alms, do you look the person in the eye?"* "Oh, I don't know. I haven't really thought about it." *The second question: "And when you give alms, do you touch the hand of the person you are giving them to, or do you toss the coin at him or her?" This is the [issue]: the flesh of Christ, touching the flesh of Christ, taking upon ourselves this suffering for the poor. Poverty for us Christians is not a sociological, philosophical, or cultural category, no. It is theological. . . . This is our poverty: the poverty of the flesh of Christ, the poverty that brought the Son of God to us through his incarnation. A poor Church for the poor begins by reaching out to the flesh of Christ.*

—Pope Francis, *The Church of Mercy*

But a Samaritan while travelling came near him; and when he saw him, he was moved with pity. He went to him and bandaged his wounds, having poured oil and wine on them. Then he put him on his own animal, brought him to an inn, and took care of him.

—Luke 10:33–34

Do you give alms? Do you have personal contact with people you are assisting?

May 1

Take Whatever Helps

To the truly humble man the ordinary ways and customs and habits of men are not a matter for conflict. The saints do not get excited about the things that people eat and drink, wear on their bodies or hang on the walls of their houses. To make conformity or nonconformity with others in these accidents a matter of life and death is to fill your interior life with confusion and noise. Ignoring all this as indifferent, the humble man takes whatever there is in the world that helps him to find God and leaves the rest aside.

—Thomas Merton, *New Seeds of Contemplation*

That's a pretty good summary of the challenges of everyday life: making good choices about the things the world presents to us—taking what helps and leaving the rest alone.

What religious "externals" are helpful to your spiritual life? How can you make better use of them?

May 2

Repentance and Forgiveness

Should anyone do anything that is disedifying, and it seems that as a result he should be held in less esteem than he was held before, let him not be so discouraged as to wish to give up, but let him humble himself and ask forgiveness of those who might have been scandalized by his bad example. He should thank God, who has permitted him to be humbled, so that he can be known by all for what he is. The brethren who behold him should think that they could fall into even greater weakness, and should ask God to strengthen them.

—St. Ignatius Loyola, *The Letters of St. Ignatius of Loyola*, William J. Young, SJ

Repentance and forgiveness are freeing. The wrongdoer doesn't have to maintain a façade of innocence. His friends don't have to feel superior, knowing that they are capable of doing the same thing.

Ask God to show you where you might be hampered by a façade of blamelessness.

May 3

Talking to People

When the Father Ignatius began speaking with someone, at first he would let the man speak as much as he wanted, and then he would speak to him in such a way that, even if the person were very imperfect, he would not be scandalized. When he would get to know the person better and the person felt more at ease, the Father would slowly proceed and, without any violence, change the whole game.

—Luis Gonçalves da Camara, SJ, in *Ignatius of Loyola: The Pilgrim Saint*, J. Ignacio Tellechea Idigoras

The mind of the wise makes their speech judicious,
and adds persuasiveness to their lips.

—Proverbs 16:23

Bring to mind an enjoyable conversation with someone you were meeting for the first time. How did the other person put you at ease? How can you do the same?

May 4

The Mystery That Is God

To speak about finding God in all things is to admit that no doctrine, no tradition and no Scripture can exhaust the mystery that is God. It is to remember that our theology, our prayer and our teaching are limited in their ability to convey this mystery, and that as a result we must ultimately stand in awe before God. We who have grown up in a pluralistic world have seen good things in people of varied backgrounds; we know that any talk of ultimate truth must be humble before the vastness of human experience and of creation.

—Tim Muldoon, "Why Young Adults Need Ignatian Spirituality," *America*

For my thoughts are not your thoughts,
nor are your ways my ways, says the LORD.
For as the heavens are higher than the earth,
so are my ways higher than your ways
and my thoughts than your thoughts.

—Isaiah 55:8–9

Lord, remind me of this—that you are greater than anything I can say or think about you.

May 5

Interruptions *Are* Life

I've come to believe that one aspect of maturity is the ability to see life's interruptions not as interruptions but as necessary events and journeys. Interruptions are *life. The unexpected is simply the life you have but don't yet know about.*

—Vinita Hampton Wright, *Days of Deepening Friendship* blog

Someone will interrupt me today—a knock at the door, a text message, a phone call, a question, an unwelcome request. This is my life. I will embrace it.

How might this observation help you respond more calmly and generously to "interruptions"?

May 6

Every Beggar Is Christ Carrying His Cross

I hold that every poor man, every vagrant, every beggar is Christ carrying his cross. And as Christ, we must love and help him. We must treat him as a brother, a human being like ourselves. If we were to start a campaign of love for the poor and homeless, we would, in a short time, do away with depressing scenes of begging, children sleeping in doorways and women with babies in their arms fainting in our streets.

—St. Alberto Hurtado, SJ, in *Alberto Hurtado: A Man After God's Heart*, Katherine Gilfeather

What would a campaign of love for those who are poor look like in my community?

Who are the poor in your community? How can you reach out to them?

May 7

Something New Will Grow

Notice those moments when we seem to be in contact with something, or someone, beyond ourselves. This could happen in all sorts of ways—through intense communion with nature or in a human relationship, in a moment of deep insight that seemed to come from beyond ourselves. When these moments happen, we could say that God has not only "touched" us but has somehow "taken root" in our lived experience. Something new will grow from that union.

—Margaret Silf, *Inner Compass*

Create in me a clean heart, O God,
  and put a new and right spirit within me.
Do not cast me away from your presence,
  and do not take your holy spirit from me.
Restore to me the joy of your salvation,
  and sustain in me a willing spirit.

—Psalm 51:10–12

Recall a time when you were touched by God deeply. Did something new grow from it? How did that happen?

May 8

Look Inward

Look not outward but within. Self-knowledge is at the root of all real religious knowledge. And this is why the beginning of true religion cannot lie in a book, or in science, or in arguing, or in listening to sermons. To look into the soul is to begin to find God. However able the sermon, however sacred the book, it will teach nothing to the person who has not started to look inward.

—Owen Chadwick, *Newman: A Short Introduction*

"The Lord does not see as mortals see; they look on the outward appearance, but the Lord looks on the heart."

—1 Samuel 16:7

What has been the benefit of getting in touch with you inner life? What helps you do this?

May 9

Daniel Berrigan, SJ

Daniel Berrigan, SJ, an American Jesuit, poet, writer, and peace activist, was born on this day in 1921. Berrigan spent several years in prison for radical nonviolent protests of the Vietnam War. He is one of the founders of the Plowshares Movement, a Christian pacifist group that protests nuclear weapons, and has been a vigorous advocate for the poor and needy. He has written thirty-five books of essays, reflections, and poetry.

He wrote:

Sometime in your life, hope that you might see one starved man, the look on his face when bread finally arrives. Hope that you might have baked it or bought it or even kneaded it yourself. For that look on his face, for your meeting his eyes across a piece of bread, you might be willing to lose a lot, or suffer a lot, or die a little, even.

—In *God in the Moment*, Kathy Coffey

> But be doers of the word, and not merely hearers who deceive themselves. Religion that is pure and undefiled before God, the Father, is this: to care for orphans and widows in their distress, and to keep oneself unstained by the world.
>
> —James 1:22, 27

Tell the Lord about your desire to help those in need. Listen to what he says.

May 10

This Isn't How It Has to Be

One cannot simply say that this is how it is and how it will always be because the world is like that—in the context of the Exercises, *that is plainly untrue. It is untrue because God does not intend that kind of arrangement of human society in which so many are excluded. These sufferings are not divinely made but humanly made. God has not abandoned creation but reaches out at all times and to all peoples with possibilities and grace for redemption of all aspects of human life.*

—Monika Hellwig, "Finding God in All Things: A Spirituality for Today"

Good news—things don't have to be this way! Find the work that God has for you and do it cheerfully, knowing that you're part of a project to change the world.

Where do you most clearly see God at work to change a distressing situation? Take some time to reflect on this.

May 11

Matteo Ricci, SJ

Matteo Ricci, SJ, the first Westerner to reach the Imperial Court of China, died on this date in 1610. Ricci is a major figure in Chinese history because he and his Jesuit colleagues brought science and Western knowledge to a land that had been isolated from the rest of the world. He adapted to Chinese culture and taught the Christian faith using concepts drawn from Confucianism.

Ricci had a generous admiration for Chinese religion:

Whence we can hope of the immense goodness of the Lord, that many of these ancients were saved in the natural law, with the special help that only God grants to those who do on their part as much as they can to receive it. This can also be derived from many beautiful books that remain to this day, of these their ancient philosophers, full of great piety and good advice for human living and acquiring virtues, in no way inferior to the most famous of our ancient philosophers.

—In "What Were 'The directives of Matteo Ricci' Regarding the Chinese Rites?" Paul A. Rule, Ph.D., *Pacific Rim Report*

And Jesus came and said to them, "Go therefore and make disciples of all nations, baptizing them in the name of the Father and of the Son and of the Holy Spirit."

—Matthew 28:18–19

Consider your encounters with people from other faiths and cultures. What have you learned from them?

May 12

A Place to Pray

Ignatius implored his companions to make not just time for intimacy, but space as well. At a time when church leadership was calling for people to come to the Temple to be seen and offer their sacrifice openly, Jesus implored his followers to go to their rooms, close the door, and pray in secret. For what is done in secret is done from the heart, the true heart. Here there is no judgment from the eyes of others. Here there is no fear, no worry, no anxiety, save those I bring here to be relieved of. Here all are worthy.

—Lisa Kelly, *This Ignatian Life* blog

In the morning, while it was still very dark, he got up and went out to a deserted place, and there he prayed.

—Mark 1:35

How do the places where you pray affect your experience of prayer?
Can you make changes that might be helpful?

May 13

Enter By Their Door

Ignatius taught not only by word, but also by example. The first thing to do is to concentrate one's heart and soul in loving the person you want to aid. Even though the person in question was a hardened sinner, he found something in him to love, his natural gifts, his belief in God, and any other good things about him. One should watch carefully for an occasion to give the conversation a religious turn. Father Ignatius used to speak of this method "entering by their door so as to come out by our door."

—Jerome Nadal, SJ, in *The Ignatian Tradition*, Kevin F. Burke, Eileen Burke-Sullivan, Phyllis Zagano

Ignatius must have been a great person to talk to. He seems to have been one of those rare people who connect immediately when you meet them. After ten minutes of conversation it seems like you've been friends for a long time.

Look for an opportunity to spend a few minutes chatting comfortably with an acquaintance you don't ordinarily talk to much.

May 14

Prayer for Light and Help

Jesus, I feel within me
a great desire to please you
but, at the same time,
I feel totally incapable of doing this
without your special light and help,
which I can expect only from you.

Accomplish your will within me—
even in spite of me.

—St. Claude de la Colombière, SJ, in *Hearts on Fire*, Michael Harter, SJ

Let us therefore approach the throne of grace with boldness, so that we may receive mercy and find grace to help in time of need.

—Hebrews 4:16

Pray the prayer for light and help. Then speak to God about it.

May 15

Life-Giving Relationships

Christian ministry and mission can never be seen as an individualistic enterprise. We always interact as members of the body of Christ. We always serve in the context of a relationship with Christ and with others. Ministry is a sharing of life and love. Ministry in the Ignatian mode is based on Jesus' promise that "where two or three are gathered together in my name, there am I in the midst of them" (Matthew 18:20).

—David L. Fleming, SJ, *What Is Ignatian Spirituality?*

So you are no longer strangers and aliens, but you are citizens with the saints and also members of the household of God.

—Ephesians 2:19

What especially touched you recently in your relationship with a coworker?

May 16

How the Pope Prays

Prayer for me is always a prayer full of memory, of recollection, even the memory of my own history or what the Lord has done in his church or in a particular parish. For me it is the memory of which St. Ignatius speaks in the First Week of the Exercises in the encounter with the merciful Christ crucified. And I ask myself: "What have I done for Christ? What am I doing for Christ? What should I do for Christ?" It is the memory of which Ignatius speaks in the "Contemplation for Experiencing Divine Love," when he asks us to recall the gifts we have received. But above all, I also know that the Lord remembers me. *I can forget about him, but I know that he never, ever forgets me. Memory has a fundamental role for the heart of a Jesuit: memory of grace, the memory mentioned in Deuteronomy, the memory of God's works that are the basis of the covenant between God and the people. It is this memory that makes me his son and that makes me a father, too.*

—Pope Francis, "A Big Heart Open to God," *America*

Seek the Lord and his strength;
seek his presence continually.
Remember the wonderful works he has done,
his miracles, and the judgments he has uttered.

—Psalm 105:4–5

Spend some extra time today reflecting on memories that you especially cherish. How do you see Christ in them?

May 17

Fit the Means to the End

In every good choice, as far as depends on us, our intention must be simple. I must consider only the end for which I am created, that is, for the praise of God our Lord and for the salvation of my soul. Hence, whatever I choose must help me to this end for which I am created.

I must not subject and fit the end to the means, but the means to the end. Many first choose marriage, which is a means, and secondarily the service of God our Lord in marriage. . . . As a result, what they ought to seek first, they seek last.

Therefore, my first aim should be to seek to serve God, which is the end, and only after that, if it is more profitable, to have a benefice or marry, for these are means to an end.

—*The Spiritual Exercises* 169

This is Ignatius's bedrock principle for making good decisions: *Seek God first.* If service of God is our goal, our choices are likely to be sound.

Are you facing an important decision? Pray that the desire to serve God will be your paramount consideration.

May 18

Good Works Enhance Prayer

One who seeks the spirit of God in good works will find it better in prayer later on than the one who seeks God first in prayer and then in action, as we often do. Whoever seeks and finds the spirit of Christ in good works makes much more solid progress than the one who seeks it in prayer alone. Let then your life be conducted in this manner, both with Martha and Mary, that is, made up of both action and contemplation . . .

—St. Peter Faber, SJ, in "The Pilgrim Journey of Ignatius," Peter Schineller, SJ

This echoes what Ignatius said about love: "love ought manifest itself in deeds rather than words" and "love consists in a mutual sharing of goods." Love is action.

Have good works enhanced prayer in your experience? How has this happened?

May 19

Know for Sure That He Is Looking at You!

How do you abide in the presence of the Lord? When you visit the Lord, when you look at the tabernacle, what do you do? Without speaking . . . "But I speak, I talk, I think, I meditate, I listen . . ." *Very good! But do you let yourself be looked at by the Lord? [May we let] ourselves be gazed upon by the Lord. He looks at us, and this is itself a way of praying. Do you allow yourselves to be gazed upon by the Lord? But how do you do this? You look at the tabernacle and you let yourselves be looked at . . . it is simple!* "It is a bit boring; I fall asleep." *Fall asleep then, sleep! He is still looking at you. But know for sure that he is looking at you!*

—Pope Francis, *The Church of Mercy*

Be strong and courageous; do not be frightened or dismayed, for the Lord your God is with you wherever you go.

—Joshua 1:9

Answer the pope's question: How do you abide in the presence of the Lord?

May 20

Ignatius Wounded in Battle

On this day in 1521, Ignatius Loyola was seriously wounded defending the city of Pamplona from assault by French forces. The city's defenders, numbering about one thousand, were crumbling under the attack by the 12,000-member French army. Ignatius rallied them, crying "Victory or death," and the Pamplonese resisted until Ignatius was wounded. As soon as he went down, the city surrendered.

Ignatius's wounds were severe. A cannonball shattered his right leg and wounded his left. The French, admiring his bravery, carried Ignatius to his family's home, where he endured two painful surgeries and spent more than a year recuperating. This time of enforced idleness was the turning point in Ignatius's life. He became aware of the ways God was leading him through the ebb and flow of his inner life, and eventually decided to devote his life to the service of God.

> You were taught to put away your former way of life, your old self, corrupt and deluded by its lusts, and to be renewed in the spirit of your minds, and to clothe yourselves with the new self, created according to the likeness of God in true righteousness and holiness.
>
> —Ephesians 4:22–24

Recall a time when you went through a significant change in your relationship with God. Spend some time savoring those memories. Speak to God about them.

May 21

Suffering Will Not Shake You

If you act on Jesus's words (not just listen but act *on them) you'll be like the fellow who builds on rock. Your life will be steady, unshaken, permanent. Notice that Jesus does* not *say that you won't encounter any storms in your life. The one who builds on rock still has to face the rains and the winds. Believing in God, and acting on Jesus's words, does not guarantee that your life will be free of suffering. But following the word of God means that the suffering will not shake you.*

—James Martin, SJ, "Kabina's Cry: Why Building a House on Rock Doesn't Mean Rain Won't Fall," *The Huffington Post*

Everyone then who hears these words of mine and acts on them will be like a wise man who built his house on rock.

—Matthew 7:24

What storms are especially troubling you right now? Hear the Lord promising that these "rains and floods and winds" will not shake you.

May 22

Our Hearts Are Our Monasteries

Every Jesuit should be able to live like a monk in the middle of the noise of the city. That means that our hearts are our monasteries and at the bottom of every activity, every reflection, every decision, there is silence, the kind of silence that one shares only with God.

—Adolfo Nicolas, SJ, Superior General's Summary 2012

Be still, and know that I am God!

—Psalm 46:10

What helps you retreat to that place of quiet where you can find God?

May 23

Formed By God's Grace

There are very few [persons] who realize what God would make of them if they abandoned themselves entirely into his hands and let themselves be formed by his grace. A thick and shapeless tree trunk would never believe that it could become a statue, admired as a miracle of sculpture, and would never submit itself to the chisel of the sculptor who sees by his genius what he can make of it.

—St. Ignatius Loyola in *The Way of Ignatius Loyola*, Philip Sheldrake

Yet, O LORD, you are our Father;
we are the clay, and you are our potter;
we are all the work of your hand.

—Isaiah 64:8

How have you already been formed by God's grace? How might this process continue?

May 24

Our Lady of the Way

Today is the feast of Our Lady of the Way, Santa Maria Della Strada, patroness of the Jesuits. Ignatius and the early Jesuits were drawn to this devotion, which honors Mary as the protector of travelers, because they saw themselves as men on the road, willing to go everywhere to serve Christ. The Church of Santa Maria della Strada in Rome was the first Jesuit mother church. The Church of the Gesu, the current Jesuit mother church, was erected on that site in 1568.

> Thomas said to him, "Lord, we do not know where you are going. How can we know the way?" Jesus said to him, "I am the way, and the truth, and the life. No one comes to the Father except through me. If you know me, you will know my Father also."
>
> —John 14:5–7

Recall your spiritual journey—the road you have travelled with Christ. What comes to mind? Spend some time with those memories.

May 25

The Crowning Glory of the Spiritual Exercises

The death of the empirical self is the crowning glory of the Spiritual Exercises: that a person's self-love, self-will, and self-interest have merged into the will and the interest and the love of Christ. As long as we can live this for a few moments, for a few hours, for a few days, we have become contemplatives in action. So it is really a mystical grace. We cannot produce it, but we can dispose ourselves for it by loving God.

—Anthony de Mello, SJ, *Seek God Everywhere*

Trust in the LORD with all your heart,
  and do not rely on your own insight.
In all your ways acknowledge him,
  and he will make straight your paths.
Do not be wise in your own eyes;
  fear the LORD, and turn away from evil.
It will be a healing for your flesh
  and a refreshment for your body.

—Proverbs 3:5–8

I want to know your mind, Lord. Show it to me. Give me the grace to know it and love it.

May 26

Now Is the Moment!

How many are the moments in which we can be Christ for others! Now is the moment: do not delay. The bridegroom is coming. Trim the wicks of your lamps. Perhaps next to you, perhaps now reading your e-mail, perhaps sleeping next to you, perhaps in the cubicle next to yours, perhaps on the other end of the classroom, perhaps on the playing field, is someone whom Christ must touch right now. And perhaps yours are the only hands, the only voice, the only smile, the only embrace, the only look that he can use to touch his beloved. Be alert! The moment will never come again. Trust yourself to God, and he will act.

—Tim Muldoon, *Dot Magis* blog

The bridegroom came, and those who were ready went with him into the wedding banquet; and the door was shut. Later the other bridesmaids came also, saying, "Lord, lord, open to us." But he replied, "Truly I tell you, I do not know you." Keep awake therefore, for you know neither the day nor the hour.

—Matthew 25:10–13

Look for the person whom Christ must touch—today!

May 27

When We Can't Have What We Want

This is a tension in human existence—the now and the not yet, the recognition of the reality of the present moment and the desires that God has deemed to place on our hearts that seem utterly impossible. Ignatius told his companions that the solution to dealing with this tension is to step back in prayer and recognize the current reality and the future desire of our heart. See them from all angles—looking for God's invitation within them. Christ sits next to us in all of these, trying desperately to get us to see that He is right here and will be here no matter what the future holds.

—Lisa Kelly, *This Ignatian Life* blog

Do you not realize that Jesus Christ is in you?

—2 Corinthian 13:5

Lord, give me the grace to consider the circumstances of life objectively—to see them from all angles, looking for your invitation in them.

May 28

Patiently Give Your Reasons

We should not dispute stubbornly with anyone; rather we should patiently give our reasons with the purpose of declaring the truth lest our neighbor remain in error, and not that we should have the upper hand.

—St. Ignatius Loyola, *The Letters of St. Ignatius of Loyola*, William J. Young, SJ

Ignatius is talking about that tug of pride when we're arguing a point. We want to *win.*

Where are you driven to seize the upper hand?

May 29

Hate the Disorder in Your Own Soul

Instead of loving what you think is peace, love other men and love God above all. And instead of hating the people you think are warmongers, hate the appetites and the disorder in your own soul, which are the causes of war. If you love peace, then hate injustice, hate tyranny, hate greed—but hate these things in yourself, not in another.

—Thomas Merton, *Passion for Peace: Reflections on War and Nonviolence*

Why do you see the speck in your neighbor's eye, but do not notice the log in your own eye?

—Luke 6:41

Ask the Holy Spirit to show you the disorders in your heart that stand in need of correction.

May 30

God Looks to See What Good We Have Done

Father Ignatius says that God deals with us differently than do worldly human beings. They look to find whatever is bad or imperfect in our actions, they take note of it and then hold it against us. God, however, looks to see what good we have done, and closes an eye to our imperfections.

—Jerome Nadal, SJ, in *Ignatius of Loyola: The Pilgrim Saint*, J. Ignacio Tellechea Idigoras

Ignatius's spiritual perspective flows from his view of what God is like. He viewed God as a giver, showering us with gifts "as the rays of light descend from the sun."

How can you imitate God as Ignatius understood him—looking to see what good others have done, and closing the eye to imperfections?

May 31

To Want What God Wants

These [people] want to rid themselves of the attachment, but they wish to do so in such a way that they desire neither to retain nor to relinquish the sum acquired. They seek only to will and not will as God our Lord inspires them, and as seems better for the service and praise of the Divine Majesty. Meanwhile, they will strive to conduct themselves as if every attachment to it had been broken. They will make efforts neither to want that, nor anything else, unless the service of God our Lord alone moves them to do so.

—*The Spiritual Exercises* 155

This meditation from the Spiritual Exercises examines the ways that people might approach the challenge of managing an unexpected fortune. The first group talks about using it for God's purposes but does nothing about it. The second group bargains with God about it. Then there is the third group—those who want only what God wants.

Consider how attachments affect your freedom. Where do you feel constrained by them?

June 1

Companions of Jesus

What is it to be a Jesuit? It is to know that one is a sinner, yet called to be a companion of Jesus as Ignatius was: Ignatius, who begged the Blessed Virgin to "place him with her Son," and who then saw the Father himself ask Jesus, carrying his Cross, to take this pilgrim into his company.

What is it to be a companion of Jesus today? It is to engage, under the standard of the Cross, in the crucial struggle of our time: the struggle for faith and that struggle for justice which it includes.

—Society of Jesus, Thirty-Second General Congregation

As you therefore have received Christ Jesus the Lord, continue to live your lives in him, rooted and built up in him and established in the faith, just as you were taught, abounding in thanksgiving.

—Colossians 2:6–7

In what circumstances do you feel that you are a companion of Jesus? What helps you feel this way?

June 2

Anthony de Mello, SJ

Anthony de Mello, SJ, a psychotherapist and spiritual director, died on this day in 1987. He was a popular spiritual writer whose books drew on his experience as a therapist and insights from the religions of his native India. His best-known book is *Sadhana—A Way to God*. These are some short sayings of his:

> *"Behold God beholding you . . . and smiling."*
>
> *"Both what you run away from—and yearn for—is within you."*
>
> *"You do not have to change for God to love you."*
>
> *"Be grateful for your sins. They are carriers of grace."*
>
> *"Say goodbye to golden yesterdays: or your heart will never learn to love the present."*
>
> *"Peace is only found in yes."*

Choose one of the short sayings and meditate on it.

June 3

Lost Children

Consider a blissfully happy couple finding all they need in one another. For no other reason than generosity and the desire to share their happiness, they decide to adopt children as their own. From then on their life undergoes a profound change. Now they are vulnerable; their happiness is wrapped up in the welfare of the children; things can never be the same again.

If the children choose to alienate themselves and start on the path to ruin, the couple are stricken. They will plead, humble themselves, make huge sacrifices, go out of themselves to get their loved ones to understand that the home is still their home, that the love they have been given is unchanging.

This perhaps gives us some insight into redemption. In a mystery we cannot fathom, God "empties," "loses" Himself in bringing back to Himself His estranged, lost children. And this is all the Father wants. This is the only remedy for His wound. God is no longer pure God, but always God-with-humanity-in-His-heart.

—Ruth Burrows, OCD, *Essence of Prayer*

But God proves his love for us in that while we still were sinners Christ died for us.

—Romans 5:8

Do you identify with the couple in the story or with the children who alienate themselves? Why?

June 4

God Is Not Absent

Sometimes God is sought as though He were absent, which is not true; He is most present in us and in all things. He is in a special way present and gives the manifestation of His presence, light and power in His commandments and in all that we are supposed to do according to our institute and calling.

—Juan de Polanco, SJ, in *Contemplation in Action*, Joseph F. Conwell, SJ

Polanco was Ignatius's secretary; he knew his mind as well as anyone. Here he expresses one of Ignatius's core ideas: that God is present in the world, not absent from it; that we can experience God in the manifold details of everyday life.

Look for God today in a place or circumstance where you haven't seen him before.

June 5

Lingering and Remembering

God's touch, though taking place in a moment of time, lives on within us forever. We can continue to let an experience of God bear fruit within us by going back to it and lingering over it. Through this remembering, lingering, and reliving process, we open ourselves to God—we allow God to move within us, to touch our hearts again so that our own experiences of God ripple deep within us and can continue to make a difference in our lives.

—Maureen Conroy, *The Discerning Heart*

This is a beautiful description of what the daily examen does for us. It allows God to touch our hearts again.

Recall a time when God blessed you greatly. Remember it in detail. Linger over these memories and savor God's goodness to you.

June 6

The Cross in Our Life

Human living offers an abundance of suffering and futility which cannot be mastered by sober courage alone. We Christians are called on to continue the sacrifice of the Lord in our lives, which alone has saving power, as the act of our faith, hope, and love. The person of the new covenant should take upon himself something of "what is lacking in Christ's afflictions" (Col 1:24). Can we say of ourselves that we carry the mark of Christ's death on us as the sign of our election?

—Karl Rahner, SJ, *Spiritual Exercises*

I am now rejoicing in my sufferings for your sake, and in my flesh I am completing what is lacking in Christ's afflictions for the sake of his body, that is, the church. It is he whom we proclaim, warning everyone and teaching everyone in all wisdom, so that we may present everyone mature in Christ.

—Colossians 1:24, 28

Reflect on this idea—that you are called to continue the suffering of Christ in your life. Have you experienced this? Does this change the way you view the sufferings in your life?

June 7

The World Is a Holy Place

By means of all created things, without exception, the divine assails us, penetrates us and molds us. We imagined it as distant and inaccessible, whereas in fact we live steeped in its burning layers. In eo vivimus *[In him we live]. As Jacob said, awakening from his dream, the world, this palpable world, to which we brought the boredom and callousness reserved for profane places, is in truth a holy place, and we did not know it.* Venite, adoremus.

—Pierre Teilhard de Chardin, SJ, *The Divine Milieu*

Remember this when all seems bleak: God is not distant, and the gloom is an illusion. God is *here*. We live in him.

Lord, open my eyes today to see the glory of your world.

June 8

Gerard Manley Hopkins, SJ

Gerard Manley Hopkins, SJ, one of the leading poets of the nineteenth century, died on this day in Dublin in 1889. His poetry is strikingly innovative, notable for its vivid imagery and new verse forms at a time when verse mainly followed traditional lines. He struggled with depression and ill health throughout his life, but his last words at age 44 were "I am so happy, I am so happy. I loved my life."

Much of Hopkins's poetry was concerned with the divine presence in the material world, as illustrated in the poem "God's Grandeur":

The world is charged with the grandeur of God.
It will flame out, like shining from shook foil;
It gathers to a greatness, like the ooze of oil
Crushed. Why do men then now not reck his rod?
Generations have trod, have trod, have trod;
And all is seared with trade; bleared, smeared with toil;
And wears man's smudge and shares man's smell: the soil
Is bare now, nor can foot feel, being shod.

And for all this, nature is never spent;
There lives the dearest freshness deep down things;
And though the last lights off the black West went
Oh, morning, at the brown brink eastward, springs—
Because the Holy Ghost over the bent
World broods with warm breast and with ah! bright wings.

—In *Hearts on Fire*, Michael Harter, SJ

Read the poem again, slowly. What comes to mind?

June 9

No Dialogue with the Devil

There can be no dialogue with the prince of this world: let this be clear! Today, dialogue is necessary among us humans, it is necessary for peace. Dialogue is an attitude that we must have among us to feel and understand each other and that dialogue must be maintained forever. Dialogue comes from charity, from love. But with that prince of this world, it is impossible to dialogue. Just as he did with Jesus, so will he do with us. "Only look," he will say, "just do this one small little scam . . . it is a small matter, nothing really"—and so he begins to lead us on a road that is slightly off. This is a pious lie: "Do it, do it, do it: there is no problem," and it begins little by little, always, no? Then he says: "But . . . you're good, you're a good person: You [get away with] it." It is flattering—and he softens us by flattery: and then, we fall into the trap.

—Pope Francis, Vatican Radio

Submit yourselves therefore to God. Resist the devil, and he will flee from you.

—James 4:7

Reflect on the pope's words. Do they ring true? How does his warning connect with your experience?

June 10

The Two Poles of Discernment

How does God call us to the right path? Usually this awareness comes through a process of discerning both the interior and the worldly poles of vocation. God's Spirit works in the depths of our humanity to help us become aware of our gifts and aspirations, and the same Spirit works through our experience to point out what the world needs from us. Often the Spirit helps us notice those problems that our talents are uniquely suited to address. Grace connects these two poles like a spark that arcs between them.

—William Spohn, SJ, "The Chosen Path," *America*

My child, if you accept my words
  and treasure up my commandments within you,
making your ear attentive to wisdom
  and inclining your heart to understanding;
if you indeed cry out for insight,
  and raise your voice for understanding;
if you seek it like silver,
  and search for it as for hidden treasures—
then you will understand the fear of the Lord
  and find the knowledge of God.

—Proverbs 2:1–5

What problems in the world draw your sympathetic attention? Might these be problems that your talents are uniquely suited to address?

June 11

Why We Get Discouraged

Our ancient enemy sets up all possible obstacles to turn us aside from the way on which we have entered. He makes use of everything to vex us. We find ourselves sad without knowing why. We cannot pray with devotion, nor contemplate, nor even speak or hear of the things of God with any interior taste or relish. He goes on to suggest that we are entirely forgotten by God our Lord and that all that we have done and all that we desire to do is entirely worthless. He thus endeavors to bring us to a state of general discouragement. We can thus see what causes our fear and weakness: it is a too-prolonged gaze at such times on our miseries.

—St. Ignatius Loyola, *The Letters of St. Ignatius of Loyola*, William J. Young, SJ

Climbing out of deep discouragement can take a long time and it can involve untangling many knots, but it begins with getting our minds off ourselves.

Does your experience of discouragement match Ignatius's analysis? How is it different? Speak to the Lord about it.

June 12

Little Things That Lift the Mind to God

An observation by one of Ignatius's close companions:

We frequently saw him taking the occasion of little things to lift his mind to God, who even in the smallest things is great. From seeing a plant, foliage, a leaf, a flower, any kind of fruit; from the consideration of a little worm or any other animal, he raised himself above the heavens and penetrated the deepest thoughts, and from each little thing he drew doctrine and the most profitable counsels for the spiritual life.

—Pedro Ribadaneira, SJ, in *Contemplation in Action*,
Joseph F. Conwell, SJ

"The kingdom of heaven is like a mustard seed that someone took and sowed in his field; it is the smallest of all the seeds, but when it has grown it is the greatest of shrubs and becomes a tree, so that the birds of the air come and make nests in its branches."

—Matthew 13:31–32

Make a point today of attending to God's presence in small things—details, gestures, tone of voice, familiar objects.

June 13

God with Us

We Christians do not have a fully satisfying explanation for why the world contains so much suffering. But we have something better: we have the power to deal *with the suffering. We know where our God is during suffering. Our God is with us: with the Jewish boy on the gallows, with Ivan Ilyich in sickness, with Job in adversity, with Paul in weakness and persecution, with Jesus in crucifixion—with us in all the senseless accidents and ruptured relationships and interior brokenness of our lives.*

—Richard J. Hauser, SJ, *Finding God in Troubled Times*

We are afflicted in every way, but not crushed; perplexed, but not driven to despair; persecuted, but not forsaken; struck down, but not destroyed; always carrying in the body the death of Jesus, so that the life of Jesus may also be made visible in our bodies. For while we live, we are always being given up to death for Jesus' sake, so that the life of Jesus may be made visible in our mortal flesh.

—2 Corinthians 4:8–11

Bring to mind a difficult situation that will not change. Imagine Christ standing with you in it.

June 14

We Don't Need Another Theory

We live in an odd time, when both workaholism and work-evasion are epidemic in our offices, assembly lines, and shop floors. Philosophers and consultants present us with one "work ethic" after another, and each theoretical house-of-cards stands for a day as a fad.

Ignatius knew—and we must learn—that what the workplace needs is not another theory, not another system, but the living presence of Jesus.

—Mike Aquilina and Kris Stubna, *Take Five: On-the-Job Meditations with St. Ignatius*

For to this end we toil and struggle, because we have our hope set on the living God, who is the Savior of all people . . .

—1 Timothy 4:10

What would "the living presence of Jesus" look like in your workplace?

June 15

An Anxious Person's Prayer

O Holy Spirit, give me stillness of soul in you.
Calm the turmoil within, with the gentleness of your peace.
Quiet the anxiety within, with a deep trust in you.
Heal the wounds of sin within, with the joy of your forgiveness.
Strengthen the faith within, with the awareness of your presence.
Confirm the hope within, with the knowledge of your strength.
Give fullness to the love within, with an outpouring of your love.
O Holy Spirit, be to me a source of light, strength and courage
so that I may hear your call ever more clearly
and follow you more generously.

—William Browning, CP, "An Anxious Person's Prayer"

"Come to me, all you that are weary and are carrying heavy burdens, and I will give you rest. Take my yoke upon you, and learn from me; for I am gentle and humble in heart, and you will find rest for your souls. For my yoke is easy, and my burden is light."

—Matthew 11:28–30

Give this prayer to someone who needs it (besides yourself).

June 16

Prayer Is Like . . .

Prayer is not a competition, or a goal-oriented activity. To pray is to already have "won." Prayer is much more like making love, or hitting a baseball, or learning to play a musical instrument (sometimes loudly and badly!), than it is like getting a promotion, or achieving a goal, or mastering a skill. Prayer is more like floating on water, than paddling stridently to get somewhere. Prayer is more "Letting Go" than "Holding On."

—Rick Malloy, SJ, *A Jesuit's Jottings* blog

"And whenever you pray, do not be like the hypocrites; for they love to stand and pray in the synagogues and at the street corners, so that they may be seen by others. Truly I tell you, they have received their reward. But whenever you pray, go into your room and shut the door and pray to your Father who is in secret; and your Father who sees in secret will reward you."

—Matthew 6:5–6

Ask the Lord to deepen your experience of prayer.

June 17

We Actually Feel This Way

Everybody hurts. When I don't have words to articulate my pain or frustration, I get crude. But crude is probably better than repressed. So I let 'em rip: Damn it. Damn. Damn. Damn it.

This is my psalm of lament: "God, damn it."

Is it too much? Or is it prayer?

The danger is that we'll ignore a simple truth: we actually feel this way. *Lament is a healthy and essential form of prayer and peacemaking. In lament we tell our God exactly how we feel, what we want . . . and we leave it for God to decide how to restore us to justice.*

—Brian Busse, SJ, *The Jesuit Post* blog

Rise up, O judge of the earth;
 give to the proud what they deserve!
O Lord, how long shall the wicked,
 how long shall the wicked exult?

—Psalm 94:2–3

What are you frustrated about? Angry about? How can these feelings have a place in your prayer?

June 18

Contemplation in Action

This Ignatian notion of contemplation in action can be understood as analogous to the kind of friendship that develops over a long time between two people. They are aware of each other even when they are apart or not engaging directly with each other. Although they may not be talking, at some deep level they are in touch with each other. Ignatius's contemplative in action has such a relationship with God. Engaging closely with God over time, we allow the Spirit to transform us into people who are more like the images of God we are created to be—that is, more like Jesus, who was clearly a contemplative in action.

—William Barry, SJ, *A Friendship Like No Other*

Contemplation in action is a paradoxical idea—detached and engaged, reflective and active. Jesus is the model.

Lord Jesus, I want to know you better. Deepen my connection with you—today.

June 19

Don't Rush It

Feelings of consolation are gifts from God. Don't rush it. The best bit of advice is spreading the "spiritual relish" thick by sitting in that moment and relishing the grace. Hold onto it. Let yourself be enveloped with consoling feelings. Ignatius says that we should relish times of consolation as a preparation for times we find ourselves in desolation. In other words, store up that "spiritual relish" for later.

—Andy Otto, *God in All Things* blog

Consolation is Ignatius's word for emotions, leadings, and other inner movements that draw us closer to God and to others. These feeling are useful for discernment, but we can also simply enjoy them.

Be attentive to feelings of consolation today. Take the time to be aware of them when they occur. Thank God for them. Enjoy them.

June 20

Many Roads to the Same Goal

Ignatius has been accused of teaching that the ends justify the means. He did not; but he did believe that there are many good ways to reach a goal, rarely just one. In any given situation one may be more effective than others in advancing God's glory and is to be preferred even if it is contrary to one's personal likes and dislikes.

—Frank Majka, SJ, "Many Roads to the Same Goal," *The Bridge* blog

Here's a related thought: we're not to condemn others who choose a road that is different from the one we prefer.

Consider a problem you are working on. Look for ways of solving it other than the way you prefer.

June 21

St. Aloysius Gonzaga, SJ

Today is the feast of St. Aloysius Gonzaga, SJ (1568–1591), who renounced the privileges of a noble family to become a Jesuit and died young caring for plague victims in Rome. Under the spiritual direction of Robert Bellarmine, SJ, Gonzaga abandoned harsh and rigid spiritual practices and grew in appreciation of God's mercy.

As he was dying, he wrote this to his mother:

The divine goodness . . . is a fathomless and shoreless ocean, and I confess that when I plunge my mind into thought of this it is carried away by the immensity and feels quite lost and bewildered there. In return for my short and feeble labors, God is calling me to eternal rest; his voice from heaven invites me to the infinite bliss I have sought so languidly. . . .

—In *Voice of the Saints*, Bert Ghezzi

But as it is written, "What no eye has seen, nor ear heard, nor the human heart conceived, what God has prepared for those who love him."

—1 Corinthians 2:9

Read the quote from St. Aloysius Gonzaga. Meditate on heaven.

June 22

Hidden Idols

We have to empty ourselves of the many small or great idols that we have and in which we take refuge, on which we often seek to base our security. They are idols that we sometimes keep well hidden; they can be ambition, careerism, a taste for success, placing ourselves at the center, the tendency to dominate others, the claim to be the sole masters of our lives, some sins to which we are bound, and many others. This evening I would like a question to resound in the heart of each one of you, and I would like you to answer it honestly: Have I considered which idol lies hidden in my life?

—Pope Francis, *The Church of Mercy*

"Why do you see the speck in your neighbor's eye, but do not notice the log in your own eye?"

—Matthew 7:3

Ask the pope's question: have you considered which idol lies hidden in your life?

June 23

Lord, Teach Us How to Pray

Prayer is not easy. It is not the speaking of many words, or the hypnotic spell of the recited formula; it is the raising of the heart and mind to God in constantly renewed acts of love. We must go forward to grapple with prayer, as Jacob wrestled with the angel. We must lift high our lamp of faith that it may show us what prayer is, and what are its power and dignity. Into the darkness we must whisper our prayer: Lord, teach us how to pray.

—Karl Rahner, SJ, *On Prayer*

"When you are praying, do not heap up empty phrases as the Gentiles do; for they think that they will be heard because of their many words. Do not be like them, for your Father knows what you need before you ask him.

Pray then in this way:

Our Father in heaven,
hallowed be your name.
Your kingdom come.
Your will be done,
on earth as it is in heaven.
Give us this day our daily bread.
And forgive us our debts,
as we also have forgiven our debtors.
And do not bring us to the time of trial,
but rescue us from the evil one."

—Matthew 6:7–13

Take some time today to pray the Lord's Prayer slowly.

June 24

Make a Good Effort and Leave the Rest to Him

If one is involved in much business, even though his intention be good and holy, he must make up his mind to do what he can, without afflicting himself if he cannot do all that he wishes. Let him do all that a man ought to do who follows the dictate of a good conscience. If other things permit, you must have patience and not think that God our Lord requires what man cannot accomplish, nor that He wishes you to be cast down. There is no need to wear yourself out, but make a competent and sufficient effort, and leave the rest to Him.

—St. Ignatius Loyola, *The Letters of St. Ignatius of Loyola,* William J. Young, SJ

At the heart of this invitation to simplicity is a surrender to God—giving back to him what he has given to us, trusting that he will provide what's necessary.

Where are you being pressured today? How can you make a good effort and leave the rest to God?

June 25

Reveal Your Heart

All should have and show great reverence, especially interior reverence, to their superiors, by considering and reverencing Jesus Christ in them; and from their hearts they should warmly love their superiors as fathers in Him. Thus in everything they should proceed in a spirit of charity, keeping nothing exterior or interior hidden from the superiors and desiring them to be informed about everything, in order that the superiors may be the better able to direct them in everything along the path of salvation and perfection.

—Constitutions of the Society of Jesus n. 551

This principle has wider application beyond religious life. To receive from others and be helped by them, we must reveal our heart. It must be done carefully and wisely, but it's necessary.

Who knows your heart best? Can you do more to open your heart to that person?

June 26

Acting "As If"

When we do not feel like believing, praying or serving in love, it is time to act as if we do *feel it. We are here in the depths of incarnational, sacramental faith. To cling to and to kiss a crucifix when we don't even feel like giving time for prayer, to reach out to the needy person when we rather feel like turning away in withdrawal are not acts of dishonesty. Rather, we are acting in line with what we deeply believe, even though, at this moment, the emotional drive for such acting is absent. This is mature faith: to act as if we are always feeling what we deeply believe.*

—George Aschenbrenner, SJ, *Stretched for Greater Glory*

This turns the tables—acting "as if" is often thought of as hypocritical and inauthentic. Actually, it's the mark of mature faith.

Apply this advice to a situation where you do not feel the confidence and hope that you believe in.

June 27

The Grace to Be Annoying

There are backseat Christians, right? Those who are well mannered, who do everything well, but are unable to bring people to the Church through proclamation and apostolic zeal. Today we can ask the Holy Spirit to give us all this apostolic fervor and to give us the grace to be annoying when things are too quiet in the Church—the grace to go out to the outskirts of life. The Church has so much need of this! Not only in distant lands, in the young churches, among people who do not know Jesus Christ, but here in the cities, in our cities, they need this proclamation of Jesus Christ. So let us ask the Holy Spirit for this grace of apostolic zeal, let's be Christians with apostolic zeal. And if we annoy people, blessed be the Lord. Onwards, as the Lord says to Paul, "take courage!"

—Pope Francis, Vatican Radio

Brothers and sisters, do not be weary in doing what is right.

—2 Thessalonians 3:13

Look for an opportunity today to show mercy and love to someone "on the outskirts of life."

June 28

The Language of the Cross

Jesus' passion brings us to embrace the world as it really is: full of violence and pain. We refuse to let religion and grace become an easy analgesic, buffering us from the real sufferings around us. Instead, we embrace whatever suffering comes into our lives. Our suffering has a meaning in "the language of the cross." We join the sufferings of the crucified Christ, the sufferings of humankind that he chose to embrace.

—Joseph Tetlow, SJ, *Making Choices In Christ*

Yet if any of you suffers as a Christian, do not consider it a disgrace, but glorify God because you bear this name. . . . Therefore, let those suffering in accordance with God's will entrust themselves to a faithful Creator, while continuing to do good.

—1 Peter 4:16, 19

In prayer today, do as Ignatius writes in the Spiritual Exercises: "As I behold Christ in this plight, nailed to the cross, I shall ponder upon what presents itself to my mind."

June 29

More Than Ever

Fr. Arrupe, superior general of the Jesuits from 1965–1983, composed this prayer after he suffered a debilitating stroke, the effects of which he patiently endured for the final ten years of his life.

More than ever I find myself in the hands of God.
This is what I have wanted all my life from my youth.
But now there is a difference;
the initiative is entirely with God.
It is indeed a profound spiritual experience
to know and feel myself so totally in God's hands.

—Pedro Arrupe, SJ, in *Hearts on Fire*, Michael Harter, SJ

And going a little farther, he threw himself on the ground and prayed, "My Father, if it is possible, let this cup pass from me; yet not what I want but what you want."

—Matthew 26:39

What comes to mind as you pray Fr. Arrupe's prayer?

June 30

Example to Others

All should take special care to guard with great diligence the gates of their senses (especially the eyes, ears, and tongue) from all disorder. In everything they should try and desire to give the advantage to the others, esteeming them all in their hearts as better than themselves [Phil. 2:3] and showing exteriorly, in an unassuming and simple religious manner, the respect and reverence befitting each one's state, in such a manner that by observing one another they grow in devotion, and praise God our Lord.

—Constitutions of the Society of Jesus 155

The purpose of this high standard for personal behavior isn't just to keep the peace among people living together. Our example is to inspire others to love God more fervently—a high standard indeed.

Whose example inspires you to greater zeal for God? What can you do to similarly inspire others?

July 1

His Divine Majesty Is Truly in All Things

They should practice the seeking of God's presence in all things, in their conversations, their walks, in all that they see, taste, hear, understand, in all their actions, since His Divine Majesty is truly in all things by His presence, power, and essence. This kind of meditation, which finds God our Lord in all things, is easier than raising oneself to the consideration of divine truths which are more abstract.

—St. Ignatius Loyola, *The Letters of St. Ignatius of Loyola*, William J. Young, SJ

This is a classic expression of one of the foundational themes of Ignatian spirituality—that God is to be found in all things. Note the practical element of this theme—that it is easier to understand and more useful than more abstract prayer.

Today, pay particular attention to finding God in two places that Ignatius mentions—in your conversations and in your walking from place to place.

July 2

An Exercise in Desire

Place before God the desires you have for yourself: expose him to all the great things you desire to do in his service. The fact that you will never actually do them, or that you feel incapable of doing them, is irrelevant. What is important is that you gladden the heart of God by showing him how immense your desires are even though your strength is very small. It is thus that lovers speak when they express the immensity of their desires which far outdistances their limited capacity.

—Anthony de Mello, SJ, *Sadhana: A Way to God*

It is a delightful notion—we can gladden God's heart by showing him our desires.

What are your greatest desires? Let your imagination have free rein. Talk to God about them.

July 3

Detachment Is the Starting Point

Usually, it's quite difficult to sort out the confusing muddle of ordered and disordered attachments that most of us live with. When does a desire to be liked and complimented become abnormal vanity? How much more money do I need? What am I willing to do to get it? We begin to answer these difficult questions by starting from a position of freedom—detachment from any particular outcome, from other people's ideas of the good life, from considerations of how someone like you should act.

—Jim Manney, *God Finds Us*

Therefore, do not worry, saying, "What will we eat?" or "What will we drink?" or "What will we wear?" For it is the Gentiles who strive for all these things; and indeed your heavenly Father knows that you need all these things. But strive first for the kingdom of God and his righteousness, and all these things will be given to you as well.

—Matthew 6:31–33

Where is detachment most difficult for you right now? Have a conversation with God about it.

July 4

A Holy Boldness

Jesuits are never content with the status quo, the known, the tried, the already existing. We are constantly driven to discover, redefine, and reach out for the magis. For us, frontiers and boundaries are not obstacles or ends, but new challenges to be faced, new opportunities to be welcomed. Indeed, ours is a holy boldness, "a certain apostolic aggressivity," typical of our way of proceeding.

—Society of Jesus, Thirty-Fifth General Congregation

This is a vision that inspires—restless, open to the new, bold, excited by challenge.

Where are you stirred by this Ignatian vision?

July 5

Make My Heart Still

Lord, take my poor heart. It is often so far from you, lost in a thousand things and in the trifles that fill up my everyday life. Lord, only you can collect the thoughts of my heart and have it concentrate on you, you who are the center of all hearts, the Lord of all souls. Only you can bestow the spirit of prayer, only your grace is able to allow me to find you amidst this multitude of things, amidst the distractions of everyday life, you, the one necessity, the one person with whom my heart can become still.

—Karl Rahner, SJ, *The Mystical Way in Everyday Life*

We can get ready to pray, but only God can give the spirit of prayer.

Pray this prayer again, slowly, paying close attention to the sense of the words. Note what comes to mind.

July 6

Scratching the Ego Itch

Sometimes our desires are in fact good indicators of where we need to go or what course we need to take. But sometimes just the opposite is true. What I want so badly may scratch an ego itch but do nothing to further my purpose in life; it might even lead me astray of my purpose. Greed, pride, or a host of other debilitating drives can take a powerful hold on us and are all the more pernicious because we're not fully aware of how deeply they may have affected our thinking. That's what Ignatius meant by an attachment to disordered affections that can undermine our judgment.

—Chris Lowney, *Heroic Living*

That's why we need discernment—to distinguish authentic desires from those that merely scratch an ego itch.

What do you most strongly desire now? What are your feelings about it? Are they strong, weak, mixed, peaceful, disturbed?

July 7

Where Are *You*?

People often ask "Where is God in my life?" The best response I can give is to ask "Where are you*?—that's where God is." In this way prayer can be something very practical and steeped in where we really live. In brief, we recognize the divine within ourselves, rather than trying to engage a God out there somewhere.*

—J.J. O'Leary, SJ, "Where Are You?"

God is *here*—in the world that I know, in my everyday experience. How wonderful!

Where do you feel the presence of God most strongly in your life right now?

July 8

A Reason for Desolation

The third reason [why God permits desolation] is because God wishes to give us a true knowledge and understanding of ourselves, so that we may have an intimate perception of the fact that it is not within our power to acquire and attain great devotion, intense love, tears, or any other spiritual consolation; but that all this is the gift and grace of God our Lord. God does not wish us to . . . attribute to ourselves the devotion and other effects of spiritual consolation.

—*The Spiritual Exercises* 322

God doesn't cause desolation but he permits it. It has a purpose—to give us understanding of ourselves.

Carefully examine a recent experience of desolation. What does it reveal about your expectations and desires?

July 9

A Great Generosity

The Exercises have the greater spiritual effectiveness the greater the humility and the less the curiosity, the greater the faith and trust that the Lord will act through them, the greater the desire for the salvation and perfection of our own souls, the greater the application and exactness, and the greater the desire for the glory and praise of Jesus Christ, with which we make them. What is of most avail in all prayer is a great generosity in surrendering to God all our powers and operations, and all that we are; and also to hope constantly, desire intensely, and beg from God that he might bring about whatever will be for his own greater glory and praise.

—Jerome Nadal, SJ, in *The Ignatian Tradition*, Kevin F. Burke, Eileen Burke-Sullivan, Phyllis Zagano

"Great generosity," "hope constantly," "desire intensely," "beg from God"—this account of Ignatian prayer is bathed in passion and fervor.

Lord, increase my zeal for you and for your work.

July 10

Ignatius Hated Selfishness

Ignatius hated selfishness. He called it "self-love," and he set it in opposition to true charity toward oneself. If we really want what is best for ourselves, we will work for the good of others. For self-love is the root cause of much sadness and dissatisfaction. Ignatius urged his followers to find the divine image in all people—even difficult people and sinners—just as they were to find God in all things. Ignatian spirituality leads us to care for the comfort of others rather than our own comfort.

—Mike Aquilina and Kris Stubna, *Take Five: On-the-Job Meditations with St. Ignatius*

Lord, make me an instrument of your peace;
Where there is hatred, let me sow love;
Where there is injury, pardon;
Where there is error, truth;
Where there is doubt, faith;
Where there is despair, hope;
Where there is darkness, light;
And where there is sadness, joy.

Recall a time when you worked hard to serve others. Reflect on that experience.

July 11

Savoring God Is What We're After

Thinking is really a pretty terrible way of encountering God. Words are even worse. I come around again and again to a deep intuition of Ignatius: sensing, savoring God is what we're after. We must taste the bread of the Eucharist. We must feel the scabbed hands of the leper, smell the deep fresh odor of the baby's skin, listen to the wind through the trees, be awestruck by the sight of the kingfisher.

—Tim Muldoon, *The Ignatian Workout*

But thanks be to God, who in Christ always leads us in triumphal procession, and through us spreads in every place the fragrance that comes from knowing him. For we are the aroma of Christ to God among those who are being saved and among those who are perishing.

—2 Corinthians 2:14–15

Pick a favorite passage from the Gospels and enter it imaginatively, using your senses.

July 12

A Mysticism of Action

The Christ of Ignatian spirituality is Christ in action, the one who went preaching through synagogues, towns and hamlets, healing and doing good. In our day Christ sends us into the turmoil of the world and tells us to seek God as we work for the good of human beings. Thus we too learn that, along with contemplative mysticism, there is also a mysticism of action in the world.

—Peter-Hans Kolvenbach, SJ, "Message to Friends and Colleagues of the Society of Jesus"

Work often seems drearily concrete—the opposite of mystical—but in the Ignatian perspective, work deepens our connection with God.

Lord, I pray that the work I do today be of help to others—and that it brings me closer to you.

July 13

The Remedy for Anxiety

Do what you can calmly and gently. Do not be disturbed about the rest, but leave to God's providence what you cannot manage yourself. God is well pleased with the earnestness and moderate anxiety with which we attend to our obligations, but He is not pleased with that anxiety which afflicts the soul, because He wishes our limitations and weakness to seek the support of His strength and omnipotence, with the trust that in His goodness He will supply what is lacking to our weakness and shortcomings.

—St. Ignatius Loyola, *The Letters of St. Ignatius of Loyola*, William J. Young, SJ

Note that Ignatius accepts "moderate" anxiety—it's normal, even useful. It's the anxiety that afflicts the soul that's troublesome, and it happens when we forget to trust God.

What are you anxious about? Is it "moderate anxiety" or "that anxiety which afflicts the soul?" Talk to God about it.

July 14

A Cry of Wonder

This is a cry of wonder accompanied by surging emotion as I pass in review all creatures. How is it that they have permitted me to live, and have sustained me in life! Why have the angels, though they are the sword of God's justice, tolerated me, guarded me, and prayed for me! Why have the saints interceded for me and asked favors for me! And the heavens, sun, moon, stars, and the elements; the fruits, birds, fishes, and other animals—why have they all been at my service! How is it that the earth did not open to swallow me up.

—*The Spiritual Exercises* 60

This "cry of wonder" comes in the middle of a series of reflections on sin during the First Week of the Spiritual Exercises. We're able to confront wrongdoing because we know that God loves us anyway. We are sinners, but we are redeemed sinners.

Give yourself over to the wonder that Ignatius speaks of.

July 15

Take a Risk

Let the risen Jesus enter your life—welcome him as a friend, with trust: he is life! If up till now you have kept him at a distance, step forward. He will receive you with open arms. If you have been indifferent, take a risk; you won't be disappointed. If following him seems difficult, don't be afraid. Trust him, be confident that he is close to you, he is with you, and he will give you the peace you are looking for and the strength to live as he would have you do.

—Pope Francis, *The Church of Mercy*

The Spirit and the bride say, "Come."
And let everyone who hears say, "Come."
And let everyone who is thirsty come.
Let anyone who wishes take the water of life as a gift.

—Revelation 22:17

Tell God that you want to experience more of him. With great confidence and joy, ask him to come.

July 16

Sensing Rather Than Thinking

Discernment is a prayerful "pondering" or "mulling over" the choices a person wishes to consider. In his discernment, the person's focus should be on a quiet attentiveness to God and sensing rather than thinking. His goal is to understand the choices in his heart*: to see them, as it were, as God might see them.*

—Charles Jackson, SJ, "What is Discernment?"
New York Religious Life blog

Trust in the LORD with all your heart,
and do not rely on your own insight.

—Proverbs 3:5

Open my heart, Lord, to see my choices as you see them.

July 17

What Are You Certain Of?

When I ask what is certain for me in life and death, knowing that everything else may be anchored in it, the answer is the love of God as known in the heart of Christ. I am uncertain of how God began to work in me or, for that matter, when—or, more bewilderingly, why. What I have realized, though, over the years, is that life makes no sense unless I recognize, like the psalmist, that God is the author of my contingent being and that I am caught up in the mystery of God's presence in my life and in the love of God's heart as seen in Jesus. I wind up humbled before the mystery of it all.

—Gary Smith, SJ, *Radical Compassion*

I am convinced that neither death, nor life, nor angels, nor rulers, nor things present, nor things to come, nor powers, nor height, nor depth, nor anything else in all creation, will be able to separate us from the love of God in Christ Jesus our Lord.

—Romans 8:38–39

What are you certain of?

July 18

Be a Seeker of God's Desire

The God we are seeking to cooperate with is a God who is involved in every nook and cranny of the world, in its hell-holes and its mini-paradises. Where do I choose to give my time and my attention and my energy, and from what do I choose to withdraw them? In Ignatian terms, an apostolically oriented spirituality demands that I learn how to live and act as a discerner of spirits and as a seeker of God's desire for me.

—Brian McDermott, SJ, "What Is Apostolic Spirituality?" *America*

Humble yourselves therefore under the mighty hand of God, so that he may exalt you in due time. Cast all your anxiety on him, because he cares for you.

—1 Peter 5:6–7

Lord, I ask for what I want—to be a seeker of your desire for this day.

July 19

Work Gives God Glory

It is not only prayer that gives God glory but work. Smiting on an anvil, sawing a beam, whitewashing a wall, driving horses, sweeping, scouring, everything gives God some glory if being in his grace you do it as your duty. To lift up the hands in prayer gives God glory, but a man with a dungfork in his hand, a woman with a slop pail, gives him glory too. He is so great that all things give him glory if you mean they should.

—Gerard Manley Hopkins, SJ, *Poems and Prose*

Prayer is a way to holiness—but so is work! This is a foundational idea in the Ignatian perspective.

Where in your work is it easiest to see God? Where is it hardest?

July 20

Maintenance for the Soul

Ignatius wrote about spirituality as a practice, a regular endeavor through which we come to build our lives on the love of God—to order our lives according to God's plan for us. Its focus, then, is not primarily ourselves but, rather, God. In naming his spiritual practices "exercises," Ignatius sought to suggest something about how we ought to approach them: as undertakings we must repeat again and again in order to progress slowly toward a goal. We can see spiritual exercises, then, as a part of regular maintenance for the soul. If we practice them, we will give ourselves the chance to know God more intimately and to know God's will for us.

—Tim Muldoon, *The Ignatian Workout*

I like the phrase *build our lives on the love of God*. It's an edifice that needs regular maintenance. It's also a process that takes time.

What can you do to strengthen the regular "maintenance of the soul" that Muldoon describes?

July 21

A Hard Prayer

We must continue to fight suffering, yet we must also be prepared to see in it a loving principle of renewal. Pain, whether mental or physical or the spiritual pain of the dark night of the soul, hurts like hell. We can't run away from it, and in it lies the possibility of redemption for ourselves and for others if we can say, "For what it's worth, take it, God, and use it. Use it to make me grow in compassion. Use it any way you will."

—Mary Craig, "Suffering—Our Human Situation"

It's not a given—pain and suffering contain the "possibility" of redemption.

Reflect on the difficulties that cause you distress and pain. Give them over to God with the prayer "Use it any way you will."

July 22

The Value of Earthly Things

In the last analysis there is nothing that cannot be integrated into the service of God in some way, and one can say without hesitation: God grows in men to the degree that their relationship to things is a more positive one, and vice versa. This point must be emphasized because man is always tempted to consider earthly things meaningless and of little value. For our relationship to God, the "other things" are absolutely necessary—they are the place of our service and worship.

—Karl Rahner, SJ, *Spiritual Exercises*

The Ignatian way is a way of joy and affirmation—properly valuing and using earthly things draws us closer to God.

Reflect on the "earthly things"—work, relationship, learning, works of art—that are especially important to your relationship with God.

July 23

Recover the Spirit of Silence

I believe that one of the primary challenges facing the Society today is that of recovering the spirit of silence. We all need a place inside ourselves where there is no noise, where the voice of the Spirit of God can speak to us, softly and gently, and direct our discernment. We need the ability to become ourselves—silence, emptiness, an open space that the Word of God can fill, and the Spirit of God can set on fire for the good of others and of the Church.

—Adolfo Nicolas, SJ, Superior General's Summary 2012

One who spares words is knowledgeable;
one who is cool in spirit has understanding.
Even fools who keep silent are considered wise.

—Proverbs 17:27–28

Spend some extra time in prayer today simply sitting in silence. Listen to God.

July 24

A Heart Hollowed Out

A cup must be empty before it can be filled. If it is already full, it can't be filled again except by emptying it out. In order to fill anything, there must be a hollowed-out space.

This is especially true of God's word. In order to receive it, we must be hollowed out. We must be emptied of the false self and its endless demands. When Christ came, there was no room in the inn. It was full. The inn is a symbol of the heart. God's word, Christ, can take root only in a hollow.

—William Breault, SJ, *A Voice Over The Water: An Invitation To Pray*

With the emptying comes a promise—the heart *will* be filled.

Lord, quiet my restless demands in my spirit for more, more, more.
Take root in my heart.

July 25

If You Are Looking for God, God Will Find You

I believe that if you are looking for God, God will find you. Ignatius of Loyola or Mother Teresa would have likewise believed that even as we are looking, and even when we mostly feel lost, God is somehow finding us, whether or not it feels that way to us. Ignatius believed (as I do) that when we set ourselves toward some worthy purpose that transcends our meager strength, we tap into a source of meaning, strength, peace, and courage that is beyond us. We come to realize, in a graced moment, that we are called to some great purpose, that we cannot do it on our own, but that we don't have *to do it on our own.*

—Chris Lowney, *Heroic Leadership*

It's a great promise: God finds us when we set ourselves to some great purpose that we can't attain by ourselves. When we reach beyond our strength, he is there.

Ask God to reveal to you the great work that satisfies the deepest desires of your heart.

July 26

How Do You Know If You Have Found God?

How do you "know" if you have found God in a moment of your day? For me it is like hitting a hard reset on my computer; it is reconnecting to my mission, to that which makes me tick and makes me seek goodness. It is the self-awareness of seeing what is truly important and needed in a situation rather than just what I want. It is the moment of gratitude for what is, and the release of the angst for what isn't. And in those moments, there is a sense of wholeness, of Oneness with Something greater than myself, with another person, or with the world around me. When I step outside of myself enough to momentarily name and celebrate that experience of Oneness, that is when I can say I find God in all things.

—Lisa Kelly, *This Ignatian Life* blog

Simple gratitude for what is—what a wonderful gift to be able to know God in this way!

Recall memories of times when you "found God." How would you describe the experience?

July 27

Blessed Rudolf Aquaviva, SJ

Today is the feast of Blessed Rudolf Aquaviva, SJ (1550–1583), who labored for four years at the court of the Muslim king at Agra, India, seeking converts to Christ. The mission failed. Shortly afterward, Aquaviva and four associates were martyred by a Hindu mob. He wrote movingly of patient hope in the face of apparent failure:

We live only by hope, though that is very uncertain whether it may not turn out rather evil than good. Ours is a very uncertain outlook as far as the King's conversion goes. Still, the Lord makes us realize that our labors are just as pleasing and acceptable to his divine majesty as if we were to obtain that for which we are striving, for God is a witness of inmost feelings and a searcher of the heart. The thought of this makes it seem to me but a few days because of the greatness of love. For day and night we are toiling at a work of great service to God.

> So we do not lose heart. Even though our outer nature is wasting away, our inner nature is being renewed day by day. For this slight momentary affliction is preparing us for an eternal weight of glory beyond all measure.
>
> —2 Corinthians 4:16–17

What has especially helped you when you've been in danger of losing hope?

July 28

It's About Intimacy

Prayer is a matter of relationship. Intimacy is the basic issue, not answers to problems or resolutions "to be better." Many of life's problems and challenges have no answers; we can only live with and through them. Problems and challenges, however, can be faced and lived through with more peace and resilience if people know that they are not alone. A man's wife will not return from the dead, but the pain is more bearable when he has poured out his sorrow, his anger, and his despair to God and has experienced God's intimate presence.

—William Barry, SJ, *Letting God Come Close*

"Come to me, all you that are weary and are carrying heavy burdens, and I will give you rest. Take my yoke upon you, and learn from me; for I am gentle and humble in heart, and you will find rest for your souls. For my yoke is easy, and my burden is light."

—Matthew 11:28–30

Speak to God about a problem that has no answer. Then listen.

July 29

Serve the Lord with Gladness

Always serve Christ the Lord with gladness, for he is the source of all welfare. Let your whole concern be only this: to cling to no one but Jesus, who can never be taken away from you. It is he that we should keep always present to us, and it is in him that each of us should look for himself and his brother.

—St. Peter Faber, SJ

Let those who desire my vindication
  shout for joy and be glad,
  and say evermore,
"Great is the LORD,
  who delights in the welfare of his servant."
Then my tongue shall tell of your righteousness
  and of your praise all day long.

—Psalm 35:27–28

Follow the words of Ignatius, "Give thanks to God our Lord for the benefits received."

July 30

What Can We Build from the Rubble?

Wisdom is making peace with the unchangeable. We have the freedom to face the unavoidable with dignity, to understand the transformational value that attitude works on suffering. Are we responsible for our unmerited suffering? The answer is no. And yes. We are not responsible for our predicament as its cause—whether it be cancer or job loss or the death of a child or spouse. But we are responsible for what we do with the effects, for what we build from the rubble that fate has made of our lives.

—William O'Malley, SJ, *God: The Oldest Question*

Therefore, to keep me from being too elated, a thorn was given to me in the flesh, a messenger of Satan to torment me, to keep me from being too elated. Three times I appealed to the Lord about this, that it would leave me, but he said to me, "My grace is sufficient for you, for power is made perfect in weakness." So, I will boast all the more gladly of my weaknesses, so that the power of Christ may dwell in me. Therefore I am content with weaknesses, insults, hardships, persecutions, and calamities for the sake of Christ; for whenever I am weak, then I am strong.

—2 Corinthians 12:7–10

What disappointment, heartache, or misfortune are you facing now? What can you build from the rubble?

July 31

St. Ignatius Loyola, SJ

Today is the feast of St. Ignatius Loyola. On July 31, 2010, readers of the blog dotMagis wrote about what they like about Ignatius:

As a woman and a Presbyterian, I think of him as an affectionate and helpful older brother.

I think his story is a fascinating one, with many ups and downs, twists and turns. It gives me hope that God can make anything out of anyone if they only let God work, as Ignatius did.

My favorite story about St. Ignatius Loyola is that he kept a picture of the Holy Family in the room he used for prayer. It is said that he used this simple picture for his daily meditation and imagined himself sitting down to dinner with the Holy Family.

I like the fact that Ignatius started on his journey by feeling he could beat other saints at the sainthood game.

Ignatius, after all that, ended up doing office duty, just like me.

St. Ignatius is the only saint with a notarized police record! If a jailbird can be converted into one of the greatest saints, then I have a chance to be converted too.

Ignatius has been a great influence on me, especially after having 4 kids (and expecting a 5th!). Finding God in all things has been such an eye-opener for me.

I love his intensity in the beginning when he grew his nails and hair and did everything with such fervor and passion. He eventually scaled things back and adjusted to where he felt God was calling him.

What do you like about Ignatius Loyola?

August 1

St. Peter Faber, SJ

St. Peter Faber, SJ, a founder of the Society of Jesus, died on this day in 1546. Faber was a theologian and a gifted preacher who worked tirelessly for the reform of the church in Germany and Portugal. An active participant in the controversies of the Reformation, he counseled Catholics to maintain good relationships with Protestants:

If we want to be of help to them we must be careful to regard them with love, to love them in deed and in truth, and to banish from our own souls any thought that might lesson our love and esteem for them. We have to win their good will so that they will love us and readily confide in us.

The man who can speak with [Protestants] on a holy life, on virtue and prayer, will do far more good for them than those who, in the name of authority, set out to confound them by sheer weight of theological argument.

—In *The Quiet Companion*, Mary Purcell

Pray St. Peter Faber's prayer for detachment:

Cast from me every evil
that stands in the way of my seeing you,
hearing, tasting, savoring, and touching you;
fearing and being mindful of you;
knowing, trusting, loving, and possessing you;
being conscious of your presence
and, as far as may be, enjoying you.

This is what I ask for myself
and earnestly desire from you. Amen.

August 2

A Narrow Focus

Jesus in Matthew's Gospel says, "How narrow is the gate that leads to life." Mistakenly, I think, we've come to believe that this is about restriction. The way is narrow. But it really wants us to see that narrowness *is the way. Our choice is not to focus on the narrow, but to narrow our focus. The gate that leads to life is not about restriction at all. It is about an entry into the expansive.*

—Greg Boyle, SJ, *Tattoos on the Heart*

What should we focus on? This is Ignatius's answer from the First Principle and Foundation: "Our only desire and our one choice should be this: I want and I choose what better leads to God's deepening life in me."

Reflect on the Gospel words "How narrow is the gate that leads to life" from Boyle's perspective: they're about entering into the expansive.

August 3

No Commonplace Achievements

When Loyola informed Portuguese Jesuits that "no commonplace achievement will satisfy the great obligations you have of excelling," he created heroic expectations that could be met only through change and innovation on a dramatic scale.

The heroism that gripped Jesuits led to radical thought patterns. So it wasn't enough for Jesuit teams in Paraguay to advocate marginally better treatment of indigenous people within the encomienda *system; they rejected the whole system to establish the radically new reduction model. The tradition of thinking outside the box began when Loyola himself jettisoned the centuries-old model of religious life to invent a completely new kind of religious company.*

—Chris Lowney, *Heroic Leadership*

Great deeds are built on an inner transformation. This is brought about by the Spiritual Exercises.

Are you trying to make marginal improvements while God is asking for something radically new?

August 4

Attention, Reverence, Devotion

Ignatius counseled his young novices to do the following.

First, bring focus to your life by taking the time to listen to others and to see what lies before you. Give your attention to what is really there. Let that person or that poem or that social injustice or that scientific experiment become as genuinely itself as it can be.

Then reverence what you see before you. If you learn to do this, Ignatius urged, then you will gradually discover devotion, the singularly moving way in which God works in that situation, revealing goodness and fragility, beauty and truth, pain and anguish, wisdom and ingenuity.

Attention, reverence, and devotion establish the process for finding God in all things.

—Howard Gray, SJ, "Ignatius's Method for Letting God Shine Through Life's Realities"

Art teachers say that learning how to draw is basically a matter of learning how to see. "Give your attention to what is really there."

Pause today and give concentrated attention to some familiar object of your daily life.

August 5

Magnanimity and Generosity

It will be very profitable for the one who is to go through the Exercises to enter upon them with magnanimity and generosity toward his Creator and Lord, and to offer Him his entire will and liberty, that His Divine Majesty may dispose of him and all he possesses according to His most holy will.

—*The Spiritual Exercises* 5

A spirit of generosity is the one requirement for someone making the Spiritual Exercises. Ignatius chooses his words carefully: we haven't yet offered ourselves fully to God, but we must want this to happen.

Holy Spirit, show me the ways that I can more generously offer myself to God.

August 6

Go Out for the Sake of the Gospel

The Church does not rest solely beneath the shadow of our steeple; rather, she embraces a vast number of peoples and nations who profess the same faith, are nourished by the same Eucharist, and are served by the same pastors. To feel that we are in communion with the whole Church, with all of the Catholic communities of the world great and small—this is beautiful! And then, to feel we are all on a mission, great and small communities alike, that we all must open our doors and go out for the sake of the Gospel. Let us ask ourselves, then, what do I do in order to communicate to others the joy of encountering the Lord, the joy of belonging to the Church?

—Pope Francis, *The Church of Mercy*

"The harvest is plentiful, but the laborers are few; therefore ask the Lord of the harvest to send out laborers into his harvest."

—Matthew 9:37–38

Ask the pope's question: what do I do in order to communicate to others the joy of encountering the Lord?

August 7

Reestablishment of the Jesuits

On this day in 1814, Pope Pius VII reestablished the Society of Jesus, forty-one years after Pope Clement XIV, under pressure from European monarchs, suppressed the order. The reasons for the Jesuits' suppression are many and complex. Jesuits had drawn the ire of the European kings because of their involvement in court politics and their opposition to some features of absolute royal rule. In the Americas, the Jesuits opposed colonial treatment of indigenous peoples and interfered with trade practices. Behind the hostility to the Jesuits was the monarchs' rivalry with the pope, who was a secular as well as a spiritual ruler.

The Jesuits survived as an order under the protection of Catherine of Russia, who refused to promulgate the papal bull of suppression.

There were about 600 Jesuits when the order was reestablished. A century later, in 1914, there were about 17,000 Jesuits.

> [B]ut those who wait for the Lord shall renew their strength,
> they shall mount up with wings like eagles,
> they shall run and not be weary,
> they shall walk and not faint.
>
> —Isaiah 40:31

Where do you need to show patience now? What can help you be patient?

August 8

Beyond Understanding

We have been taught to study the Word of God, and of course it's right to do this. But there is a time, too, for recognizing that our heads can never grasp the truths of God, and that our purpose in prayer is not to defend or condemn ourselves or to come up with any kind of analysis or sermon, but simply to respond, from our inmost depths, to what God is sharing with us of himself.

—Margaret Silf, *Inner Compass*

To respond to God we must first hear God and notice his presence. The daily examen and other methods of Ignatian prayer help us do this.

Lord Jesus, I want to follow you and know you more intimately. Show me how to respond to your love.

August 9

Pray with Your Calendar

Does God ask that we set aside all the current realities of our world, our life, and our self? Where could we have gotten that idea?

Some great pray-ers pray with their calendar. They consider what they have done for God, and what they are doing now. They look to do for God. What better prayer is there than that?

—Joseph Tetlow, SJ, *Choosing Christ in the World*

Ignatius on the examen: "I should go over one hour after another, one period after another."

Pray the examen with your calendar at hand. Look at what happened yesterday. Look at your calendar when you ask God's help for the day ahead.

August 10

Savvy about Feelings

Prayer has made me much more savvy about the way my feelings work. Following Ignatius's advice about feelings in the Spiritual Exercises has made me back away from giving too much credence to any particular feeling at any particular time. Perhaps I feel bad now. Okay, that happens, as much as in any pilgrimage there are rainy days walking uphill. No need to be bothered by that.

Am I still growing as the person God has created me to be? Am I still willing to risk the demands of love? The feelings will follow.

—Tim Muldoon, "Savvy about Feelings," *Dot Magis* blog

Let us not grow weary in doing what is right, for we will reap at harvest time, if we do not give up.

—Galatians 6:9

Reflect on Muldoon's question: am I still growing as the person that God has created me to be?

August 11

Our Way of Proceeding—A Prayer

Lord, meditating on "our way of proceeding," I have discovered that the ideal way of our *way of acting is* your *way of acting.*

Give me that sensus Christi *that I may feel with your feelings, with the sentiments of your heart, which basically are love for your Father and love for all men and women.*

Teach me how to be compassionate to the suffering, to the poor, the blind, the lame and the lepers.

Teach us your way so that it becomes our way today, so that we may come closer to the great ideal of Saint Ignatius: to be companions of Jesus, collaborators in the work of redemption.

—Pedro Arrupe, SJ, Thirty-Fourth General Congregation

This prayer expresses one of Ignatius's strongest convictions—that when we know Christ intimately, we will know what to do.

Bring to mind a difficulty that is weighing on you. Pray for the grace to view it as Christ does, "to feel with your feelings."

August 12

A Beginner's Mind

Buddhists talk a lot about having a beginner's mind. Having a beginner's mind means doing things as if you were doing them for the first time. So when you eat, eat as if you were eating for the first time; when you pray, pray as if you were praying for the first time. When you receive the Eucharist, receive it as if you were receiving it for the first time. It opens you up to experience the Divine in all sorts of surprising places.

—Paul Coutinho, *How Big Is Your God?*

From now on, therefore, we regard no one from a human point of view; even though we once knew Christ from a human point of view, we know him no longer in that way. So if anyone is in Christ, there is a new creation: everything old has passed away; see, everything has become new!

—2 Corinthians 5:16–17

Try adopting a "beginner's mind" as you go about your daily tasks, especially as you do routine things that you've done many times before.

August 13

The Pearl of the Poor

The pearl of the poor has helped me pass into a deeper conversion, to examine myself against the prevailing values that our culture holds out to me, and to see where I most authentically live out my heart. St. Ignatius wanted members of the Society of Jesus to be poor—and therefore to serve the poor—because he knew that in their midst we would learn what real detachment is, what freedom to respond to God can mean, what humility can do to our hearts, and how we can be transformed by an experience of deep reliance on God.

—Gary Smith, SJ, *Radical Compassion*

When he came to Nazareth, where he had been brought up, he went to the synagogue on the sabbath day, as was his custom. He stood up to read, and the scroll of the prophet Isaiah was given to him. He unrolled the scroll and found the place where it was written:

"The Spirit of the Lord is upon me,
  because he has anointed me
  to bring good news to the poor.
He has sent me to proclaim release to the captives
  and recovery of sight to the blind,
  to let the oppressed go free,
to proclaim the year of the Lord's favor."

—Luke 4:16–19

What might you do to serve the poor? Ask God about this.

August 14

What Do You Really Want?

There's a question that Ignatius would have us continually ask of ourselves: What do you really want? *Peel away the layers of desires, fears, ambitions, and dreams and get in touch with the deepest desire of your heart. Ignatius believed that when you touch what the poet Hopkins called the "dearest, freshness, deep-down things," you'll find God there.*

What an optimist!

—Jim Manney, "What do you Really Want?" *Dot Magis* blog

Optimism doesn't mean perpetual cheerfulness. Ignatian optimism is the bedrock conviction that God is always loving us, always inviting us to receive more of his love.

Ask God to show you what will give you the deepest joy and the greatest satisfaction.

August 15

The Companions' First Vows

On this day in 1534, Ignatius and six companions made private vows to join together in service of the Lord. The Jesuit order was not formally established until 1541, but many Jesuits, including several of the first companions, regard this event as the day the Society was founded.

The companions professed their vows at Mass in a chapel on the hill of Montmartre, outside Paris. All were students at the University of Paris who had fallen under the influence of Ignatius Loyola. They had all come to a decision to devote their lives to God's service through an experience of the Spiritual Exercises directed by Ignatius.

The seven companions agreed to live in poverty and chastity, help souls, and go on a pilgrimage to the Holy Land. Ignatius added the condition that they would go to Rome and place themselves at the pope's disposal if the Holy Land pilgrimage proved impossible. That is what happened—they went to Rome several years later and formed the Society of Jesus.

> And everyone who has left houses or brothers or sisters or father or mother or children or fields, for my name's sake, will receive a hundredfold, and will inherit eternal life. But many who are first will be last, and the last will be first.
>
> —Matthew 19:29–30

Spend some time giving thanks to God for the great blessings that have flowed from the Jesuit order.

August 16

Speak Up or Keep Silent?

We may often have to control the desire we feel and speak less of the things of God our Lord; at other times we may speak more than the satisfaction or movement we feel prompts us to. We must proceed for the purpose of helping others, like a man who is crossing a ford. If I find a good footing—that is, some way or hope of profiting the neighbor—I will pass right on. But if the ford is muddied or disturbed and there is danger that scandal may be taken from what I say, I will rein in and seek an occasion more favorable to what I have to say.

—St. Ignatius Loyola, *The Letters of St. Ignatius of Loyola*, William J. Young, SJ

"Timing is everything"—it applies to romance, politics, hitting a baseball, and many other areas of life, including our efforts to help others grow deeper in their love of God.

Lord, show me when to speak and when to keep silent. Make me sensitive to your leading.

August 17

God Is Trying to Catch Our Attention

The Ignatian Exercises rest on the assumption that God creates this universe precisely in order to invite other persons into the relational life of the Trinity. Ignatius presupposes that at every moment of our existence God is communicating to us who God is and who we are in God's sight. Whether we are aware of it or not, at every moment of our existence we are encountering God, Father, Son, and Holy Spirit, who is trying to catch our attention.

—William Barry, SJ, *Finding God in All Things*

Long ago God spoke to our ancestors in many and various ways by the prophets, but in these last days he has spoken to us by a Son, whom he appointed heir of all things, through whom he also created the worlds. He is the reflection of God's glory and the exact imprint of God's very being, and he sustains all things by his powerful word.

—Hebrews 1:1–3

Lord Jesus, let me see you in my work today. I want to be aware of your presence and your love—in large things and in small.

August 18

St. Alberto Hurtado, SJ

Today is the feast of St. Alberto Hurtado, SJ (1901–1952), a Chilean Jesuit who served the poor. He founded the Trade Union Association of Chile, and Hogar de Cristo, an organization for poor and abandoned young people.

He wrote:

Christ roams through our streets in the person of so many of the suffering poor, sick and dispossessed, and people thrown out of their miserable slums; Christ huddled under bridges, in the person of so many children who lack someone to call father, who have been deprived for many years without a mother's kiss on their foreheads . . . Christ is without a home! Shouldn't we want to give him one, those of us who have the joy of a comfortable home, plenty of good food, the means to educate and assure the future of our children? "What you do to the least of me, you do to me," Jesus said.

> "Lord, when was it that we saw you hungry and gave you food, or thirsty and gave you something to drink? . . ." And the king will answer them, "Truly I tell you, just as you did it to one of the least of these who are members of my family, you did it to me."
>
> —Matthew 25:37, 40

Whom can you serve today in your circle of family, friends, and colleagues?

August 19

A Person Made of Light

Suppose there were a reality faster than light, so superenergized that it would be at rest, everywhere at once. Every object we see—though it appears rock-hard—is actually just another form of energy: $e = mc^2$*. Couple that with all we know from religion; encounters with God are so often described as burning bushes and fiery pillars and tongues of flame. I Am is the pool of energizing existence out of which everything draws its "is," "the dearest freshness deep down things." It may not help everyone, but when I pray, I pray to a Person made of light.*

—William O'Malley, SJ, *God: The Oldest Question*

Ignatius also imagined God as light. He urged us to contemplate all our blessings and gifts "descending from above, as the rays of light descend from the sun." The sun *is* light. God *is* blessings and gifts.

Reflect on O'Malley's image of God as light. Visualize God's blessings surrounding you as rays of light from the sun.

August 20

A God Who Works

*The God of Ignatian spirituality is the God who "acts in the manner of one who is laboring" (*Spiritual Exercises, *236). Ignatius speaks of God dwelling and at work in all creatures, in all plant and animal life, and in us. He does not speak of God pulling strings like a cosmic puppeteer, nor of a* Deus ex machina *who makes all things right at the end of a melodrama. The self-giving God of Ignatian spirituality works within the universe, within human hearts and lives, giving men and women the strength to give of themselves.*

—Ronald Modras, *Ignatian Humanism*

Our mental picture of God matters greatly. Do we think of God as angry? Loving? Distant? Forgiving? Critical? Ignatius saw God as a worker—busy, active, laboring to save and heal our world.

How do you imagine God? How does this affect your prayer?

August 21

Better Beholders

Perhaps our prayer, our liturgy, our moral action, our practices of discernment—perhaps all these are simply the practices that make us ready to behold the opportunities to love. Perhaps the Christian life is about becoming better beholders, better able to see the lightning flashes of divine grace that erupt underneath the flesh of those around us.

—Tim Muldoon, "Better Beholders," *Dot Magis* blog

"Noticing" is a key theme in Ignatian spirituality. Ignatius was a great "noticer." His conversion took off when he noticed how God was working in him. The prayer techniques he favored are those that help us "see" what God is doing.

Make a habit of praying the examen regularly, noticing where God has been active in your life.

August 22

The Spirit of God Is Peaceful

Sometimes we are interiorly anguished; and though this spirit may speak what is true, reproving us for our many failures, nevertheless if it robs us of our tranquility it is not the good spirit. The spirit of God is peaceful and gentle, even in reproof.

—St. Peter Faber, SJ, in *The Ignatian Tradition*, Kevin F. Burke, Eileen Burke-Sullivan, Phyllis Zagano

This is an important principle in the Ignatian discernment of spirits: we can know the source of a spirit by the feelings it produces. Bitter, anguished self-criticism is not from God.

Lord, give me wisdom to distinguish your voice from that of the enemy.

August 23

Find the Gold in the Opportunities at Hand

No mission is motivating until it is personal. And it is sustainable only when one makes the search for magis *a reflexive, daily habit. A* magis*-driven leader is not content to go through the motions or settle for the status quo but is restlessly inclined to look for something more, something greater. Instead of wishing circumstances were different,* magis*-driven leaders either make them different or make the most of them. Instead of waiting for golden opportunities, they find the gold in the opportunities at hand.*

—Chris Lowney, *Heroic Leadership*

Whatever your task, put yourselves into it, as done for the Lord and not for your masters.

—Colossians 3:23

What circumstance in your life might be one of these golden opportunities? Talk to God about it.

August 24

Persevere in Patience

When one is in desolation, he should strive to persevere in patience. This reacts against the vexations that have overtaken him. Let him consider, too, that consolation will soon return.

—*The Spiritual Exercises* 321

Ignatius shows insight into human psychology here. Often when we're in desolation we feel as if the bad times will never end. But they will; gloom doesn't last. (Neither does jubilation.)

Where do you need to exercise patience? Have a conversation with God about it.

August 25

Risk a Few Accidents

I far prefer a Church that has had a few accidents to a Church that has fallen sick from being closed. Go out, go out! Think of what the book of Revelation says as well. It says something beautiful: that Jesus stands at the door and knocks, knocks to be let into our heart (see Rev. 3:20). This is the meaning of the book of Revelation. But ask yourselves this question: how often is Jesus inside and knocking at the door to be let out, to come out? And we do not let him out because of our own need for security, because so often we are locked into ephemeral structures that serve solely to make us slaves and not free children of God.

—Pope Francis, *The Church of Mercy*

> Rejoice always, pray without ceasing, give thanks in all circumstances; for this is the will of God in Christ Jesus for you. Do not quench the Spirit.
>
> —1 Thessalonians 5:16–19

Reflect on this reading for a while. Does the idea of risking accidents excite you or worry you?

August 26

God and Humanity Are Not Rivals

God and humanity are not rivals. One does not love God less by loving someone more; in reaching out to love another person, we are reaching out for God. To speak about love for God and love for human beings is to speak of the same reality.

—Ronald Modras, *Ignatian Humanism*

"Teacher, which commandment in the law is the greatest?" He said to him, "'You shall love the Lord your God with all your heart, and with all your soul, and with all your mind.' This is the greatest and first commandment. And a second is like it: 'You shall love your neighbor as yourself.'"

—Matthew 22:36–39

Reach out in love today to someone you haven't heard from in a while.

August 27

Be Generous with Your Time

In business matters be generous with your time; that is, if you can, do today what you promise to do tomorrow.

—St. Ignatius Loyola, *The Letters of St. Ignatius of Loyola*, William J. Young, SJ

This advice isn't about impressing people with your diligence and efficiency. It's about being generous—putting yourself at the disposal of others.

Ask the Lord to show you how can you be generous with your time today.

August 28

Warmth of Charity for God

Each should strive to carry over the Society's prayer and contemplation to the ministries he performs, which are all spiritual: preaching, expounding Scripture, teaching Christian doctrine, giving the Exercises, hearing confessions, administering Holy Communion, and attending to other good works. In these ministries they should find God with peace, tranquility, and application of the inner person; with light, joy, satisfaction, and warmth of charity for God. And thus they should seek the same in all other ministries.

—Jerome Nadal, SJ, in *The Ignatian Tradition*, Kevin F. Burke, Eileen Burke-Sullivan, Phyllis Zagano

Note the connection between prayer and work: Work draws us into love of God; the God we meet in prayer draws us into active service.

What aspect of this reading catches your attention? Reflect on it.

August 29

Two Exercises in Gratitude

Go through a day—or through a single hour—and discipline yourself to attend to each moment as it comes and to note what is praiseworthy in that moment. Try to build this habit of dwelling completely in the moment at hand rather than in the past or future.

Choose a natural process to enter more intentionally. You might try eating much more slowly and mindfully, thoroughly tasting the food. Or you could notice, over the next few nights, what your process is like for falling asleep. Allow yourself to enjoy the natural tension and release of ordinary processes in your life.

—Vinita Hampton Wright, *Days of Deepening Friendship* blog

Gratitude is prayer. Ignatius wrote, "Give thanks to God our Lord for the benefits received."

Do one of these exercises today, and the other tomorrow.

August 30

The I-Want-It-So-Badly Virus

Sometimes we're driven by the I-want-it-so-badly virus: I so wanted to get to the top of the company, or to attract that attractive person, or to be rich, or to be recognized as important, or to have the best house, or to have a more exciting life. In fact, we sometimes delude ourselves into thinking that the object of our affection (the job, the car, the partner, the house) must be right for us precisely because we want it so badly.

—Chris Lowney, *Heroic Living*

Your proud heart has deceived you,
you that live in the clefts of the rock,
whose dwelling is in the heights.
You say in your heart,
"Who will bring me down to the ground?"

—Obadiah 1:3

Where does the I-want-it-so-badly virus afflict you?

August 31

How to Converse with People

Advice from Ignatius, writing to Jesuits participating in the Council of Trent:

> **Be prudent.** *"When speaking in any conversation, do not think you are talking in private, but in public, so as to measure your words, and to say nothing you would not wish everyone to know."*
>
> **Know your audience.** *"In the method of teaching Catechism to children suit yourselves to their age, so as to sweetly teach them the mysteries of our faith, and explain them according to the capacity and condition of your hearers."*
>
> **Be gentle.** *"Soften down the laws and prescriptions of the* Exercises *when needful, and especially for those who have to go through them in their entirety."*
>
> **Adjust your tone.** *"In discussions and arguments it is well to be brief; in order, however, to get men to follow virtue and to flee from vice, your speech should be long, and full of charity and kindness."*
>
> —In *St. Ignatius Loyola and the Early Jesuits*, Stewart Rose

Conduct yourselves wisely toward outsiders, making the most of the time. Let your speech always be gracious, seasoned with salt, so that you may know how you ought to answer everyone.

—Colossians 4:5–6

Reflect on Ignatius's counsel. Which piece of guidance seems especially pertinent to you? Why?

September 1

Pray for What You Want

Desire is a primary way that God leads people to discover who they are and what they are meant to do. The deep longings of our hearts are our holy desires. Not only desires for physical healing, but also the desires for change, for growth, for a fuller life. And our deepest desires, those desires that lead us to become who we are, are God's desires for us. They are ways that God speaks to you directly, one way that, as Ignatius says, the Creator deals with the creature.

That is why St. Ignatius asks us repeatedly in the Spiritual Exercises *to pray for what we want. It reminds you of the importance of* asking *for things in the spiritual life, and of realizing that whatever we receive is a gift from God.*

—James Martin, SJ, "Advent and Desire: A Meditation," *America*

"Ask, and it will be given to you; search, and you will find; knock, and the door will be opened for you. For everyone who asks receives, and everyone who searches finds, and for everyone who knocks, the door will be opened. Is there anyone among you who, if your child asks for bread, will give a stone? Or if the child asks for a fish, will give a snake? If you then, who are evil, know how to give good gifts to your children, how much more will your Father in heaven give good things to those who ask him!"

—Matthew 7:7–11

What do you want today? Ask God for it.

September 2

Silent Messengers

All around us, Providence has placed hosts of silent messengers who can lead us without effort by paths of love to the holy springs of peace. Water, wood, fishes, the morning dew, the cock crowing at dawn, should all be able to inspire our prayer. Clothes and flowers, perfumes and pearls, the wind whistling past, the bread on the table, the jug, chair and roof—all these things have been sanctified, all these things have been loaded with blessings and divine inspiration by the Word.

—Pierre Charles, *The Prayer of All Things*

When I look at your heavens, the work of your fingers,
the moon and the stars that you have established;
what are human beings that you are mindful of them,
mortals that you care for them?

—Psalm 8:3–4

Carry this thought into the day: everything that happens to you today has the potential of revealing God's presence to you.

September 3

Look at the Feeling

Be explicitly aware of what is going on when you are in spiritual desolation. Name it to yourself. Recall its source and tendency. It will help here to be aware of a general principle about human psychology—that reflectively attending to our own affective experiences tends to weaken their hold on us, while attending to the object *of affective acts or the ground of affective feelings tends to strengthen them. Thus, attending to the objects of anger or lust tends to intensify them; reflectively attending to the affections themselves tends to weaken them.*

—Jules J. Toner, SJ, *Spirit of Light or Darkness?*

This is a very useful principle. Look at the feeling, not at the cause of the feeling: Why am I angry? Not, why did that person say that nasty thing?

Recall a resentment you felt recently. How might this principle apply to it?

September 4

Ignatius Reaches Jerusalem

Ignatius Loyola arrived in Jerusalem on this day in 1523. The former soldier had decided to make a pilgrimage to the Holy Land after his conversion. He thought he would spend the rest of his life there working to convert Muslims.

The Franciscans in Jerusalem, who had authority over pilgrims, told him to go home, fearing that a nobleman like Ignatius would be abducted and held for ransom by Muslim warlords. Ignatius reluctantly complied and returned to Spain, where he decided to get a theological education so that he could teach about the faith. To prepare, the thirty-three-year-old Ignatius entered school with young boys in order to learn Latin.

> When you search for me you will find me; if you seek me with all your heart.
>
> —Jeremiah 29:13

Recall a decision that didn't have the result you foresaw. What came of it? Was it a dead end?

September 5

This Is the Moment

There is not a moment in which God does not present Himself, under the cover of some pain to be endured, some consolation to be enjoyed, or of some duty to be performed.

—Jean-Pierre de Caussade, SJ, *Abandonment to Divine Providence*

A maxim that wonderfully expresses the essence of the Ignatian outlook—God is found in all things; we love God by doing deeds of love.

Lord, show me your face today in the people I meet, in the work I do, in the joys and sorrows that I feel in my heart.

September 6

The Trouble Lies Within

Ignatius writing to a troubled Jesuit:

You are mistaken in thinking that the cause of your disquiet is due to the place, or your superiors, or your brethren. This disquiet comes from within and not from without. You could change residence, superiors, and brethren, but if you do not change the interior man, you will never do good. And you will everywhere be the same, unless you succeed in being humble, obedient, devout, and mortified in your self-love. This is the only change you should seek.

—St. Ignatius Loyola, *The Letters of St. Ignatius of Loyola,* William J. Young, SJ

The trouble lies within—as does the joy and the opportunity. This is a cardinal tenet of the Ignatian outlook.

Consider a conflict you're in—a troubled relationship or a project full of worry. What can you change inside that would make it go better?

September 7

Nothing Owns Me Except God

For Ignatius the foundational human experience was freedom: freedom from all created reality and freedom for God's ownership over a person's life. This kind of spiritual balance—freedom from and freedom for—he called "indifference." Ignatian indifference does not mean an absence of feeling, affection, pleasure, or care. It does mean that nothing ultimately owns me except God.

—Howard Gray, SJ, in *As Leaven in the World*, Thomas M. Landy

This is a good description of the often-misunderstood idea of Ignatian indifference—it's the freedom to be possessed by God.

Lord, show me the place of balance where I am free to want only you.

September 8

What If I Should Do What Ignatius Did?

We are challenged by Ignatius in much the same way that he was challenged by Francis and Dominic. And that may be the best purpose for books of saints: to have our complacency and mediocrity goaded, and to highlight our lame urge to go forward with the familiar rather than the difficult and serious. I feel compelled to ask, What if I should do what Ignatius did? And it does not seem to me easy to accomplish.

—Ron Hansen, "The Pilgrim: Saint Ignatius Loyola"

If it was easy, everyone would do it. That's the challenge of Ignatius and all the saints.

Which saint challenges you? Reflect on this saint's life.

September 9

St. Peter Claver, SJ

Today is the feast of St. Peter Claver, SJ (1581–1654). Born into a prosperous Spanish family, he spent his life as a Jesuit working with African slaves in Colombia, becoming the patron of African missions and interracial justice.

He worked from 1616 to 1650 in the slave port of Cartagena, where some 10,000 African slaves arrived each year. When a ship arrived, Peter first begged for fruits, biscuits, or sweets to bring to the slaves. He then went on board with translators to bring his gifts as well as his skills as a doctor and teacher. Claver entered the holds of the ships and would not leave until every person received a measure of care. Peter gave short instruction in the Catholic faith and baptized as many as he could. In this way he could prevail on the slave owners to give humane treatment to fellow Christians. He baptized more than 300,000 slaves by 1651, when he was sickened by the plague.

He said about his ministry, "We must speak to them with our hands by giving, before we try to speak to them with our lips."

> Has not God chosen the poor in the world to be rich in faith and to be heirs of the kingdom that he has promised to those who love him?
>
> —James 2:5

Reach out today to someone who is suffering in some way.

September 10

Love Our Brothers and Sisters

One of the things which we must be very firm about, if we are to please our Lord, is to cast far from us everything that could remove us from the love of our brethren. We should make every effort to love them, for Supreme Truth has said: This is how all will know you are my disciples.

—St. Ignatius Loyola, *The Letters of St. Ignatius of Loyola*, William J. Young, SJ

Above all, maintain constant love for one another, for love covers a multitude of sins. Be hospitable to one another without complaining. Like good stewards of the manifold grace of God, serve one another with whatever gift each of you has received.

—1 Peter 4:8–10

Bring to mind people whom you find difficult to love. Pray for them. Ask the Holy Spirit to show you how to love them.

September 11

Open Hands

There are many things in my life to which I cling as with a clinched fist—my possessions for sure but the immaterial things as well—the work I do, the position I hold, the friends I have, my ideas, my principles, my image. If I should open my fist, they still remain. Nothing drops out. But my hands are open. And that is what prayer is.

After a while, if I am willing to remain long enough with open hands, the Lord will come. The Lord may take something out, and he may put something in. I have only to open my heart and my hands and just stay there long enough for the Lord to come.

—Peter van Breemen, SJ, *As Bread That Is Broken*

Since there will never cease to be some in need on the earth, I therefore command you, "Open your hand to the poor and needy neighbor in your land."

—Deuteronomy 15:11

Meditate on the image of open hands. Open your hands, which hold everything that you treasure. Offer all this to the Lord.

September 12

Optimists Committed to the Long Haul

As laborers in the vineyard, we make a difference in this world. We are involved in a living and life-giving project, a constructive task whose goal is to bear fruit for the Lord. We do not work alone. We are co-workers with God. We are here to tend the garden and bear fruit that will last. One who works in a vineyard is an optimist, a laborer committed to the long haul, to patient, respectful, cooperation with fellow laborers and with the Lord of the harvest.

—Peter Schineller, SJ, *The Pilgrim Journey of Ignatius*

Two are better than one, because they have a good reward for their toil. For if they fall, one will lift up the other; but woe to one who is alone and falls and does not have another to help.

—Ecclesiastes 4:9–10

Pray for your coworkers. Consider how your relationships with them can be strengthened.

September 13

A Church That Is Poor and for the Poor

I want a Church that is poor and for the poor. They have much to teach us. Not only do they share in the sensus fidei, *but in their difficulties they know the suffering Christ. We need to let ourselves be evangelized by them. The new evangelization is an invitation to acknowledge the saving power at work in their lives and to put them at the center of the Church's pilgrim way. We are called to find Christ in them, to lend our voice to their causes, but also to be their friends, to listen to them, to speak for them, and to embrace the mysterious wisdom that God wishes to share with us through them.*

—Pope Francis, *The Church of Mercy*

Bear one another's burdens, and in this way you will fulfill the law of Christ.

—Galatians 6:2

A question for reflection: how have you found Christ in people who are poor and suffering?

September 14

What Is God's Plan?

For Ignatius, God's will isn't a precise blueprint, but it's not a vague "whatever you want" blank check either. God has a "plan" in the sense that he has an idea of the kind of person you can be and an idea of the life that would bring you most joy. The broad outlines of his idea are the same for everyone—to love and serve God and neighbor. But the particulars are unique to each of us. Finding God's will means discovering the way of life that we were meant to live.

—Jim Manney, *God Finds Us*

And we urge you, beloved, to admonish the idlers, encourage the fainthearted, help the weak, be patient with all of them. See that none of you repays evil for evil, but always seek to do good to one another and to all. Rejoice always, pray without ceasing, give thanks in all circumstances; for this is the will of God in Christ Jesus for you.

—1 Thessalonians 5:14–18

What is your idea of God's "plan"? Has it changed over time?

September 15

Suffering with Others

The Third Week meditations on Christ's Passion [in the Spiritual Exercises] teach us how difficult acceptance is. When we cannot change a situation, we are tempted to walk away from it. We might literally walk away; we are too busy to sit with a suffering friend. Or we walk away emotionally; we harden ourselves and maintain an emotional distance. We might react to the gospel accounts of Jesus' passion and death this way. They describe something terrible and horribly painful, yet we might shield ourselves from the pain. We know *the story of the Passion. Ignatius wants us to* experience *it as something fresh and immediate. We learn to* suffer with *Jesus, and thus learn to* suffer with *the people in our lives.*

—David L. Fleming, SJ, *What Is Ignatian Spirituality?*

"This is my commandment, that you love one another as I have loved you. No one has greater love than this, to lay down one's life for one's friends."

—John 15:12–13

Read the account of Jesus' Passion in John—chapters 18 and 19. Meditate on it. Allow the Lord to speak to you in the words of scripture.

September 16

Feelings Front and Center

I observe more clearly than ever certain evident signs for proceeding in the Exercises: how important it is for the discernment of spirits to see if we are attentive to ideas and reflections or rather to the Spirit itself, which appears through desires, motions, ardor or despondency, tranquility or anxiety, joy or sorrow, and other analogous spiritual motions. For it is in these motions much more easily than in thoughts that one can pass judgment on the soul and its quests.

—St. Peter Faber, SJ, in *The Way of Ignatius Loyola*, Philip Sheldrake

Ignatian discernment is about feelings, not thoughts. This is a basic concept of Ignatian spirituality.

Recall the strongest feeling that you had in the past day. Reflect on it. What does it tell you about God in your life?

September 17

St. Robert Bellarmine, SJ

Today is the feast of St. Robert Bellarmine, SJ (1542–1621), a Doctor of the Church and one of the most important leaders of the Catholic Reformation. He was a cardinal, one of the most powerful men in Rome, but he lived an austere life and gave most of his money to the poor. He once gave the tapestries from his living quarters to the poor, saying that the walls wouldn't catch cold.

He wrote:

What various powers lie hidden in plants! What strange powers are found in stones, especially magnetic stones and amber. What strength do we see in animals, such as lions, bears, bulls and elephants. How clever, although tiny, are ants, spiders, bees and flies. How great is human genius, which has invented skills such that we wonder whether nature surpasses art or art surpasses nature! Now lift up your eyes to God, my soul, and reflect on how great is the strength, efficacy, and power of the Lord your God.

"But ask the animals, and they will teach you;
the birds of the air, and they will tell you;
ask the plants of the earth, and they will teach you;
and the fish of the sea will declare to you.
Who among all these does not know
that the hand of the LORD has done this?"

—Job 12:7–9

Do what Bellarmine suggests: look at the natural world and "reflect on how great is the strength, efficacy, and power of the Lord your God."

September 18

If You Can Talk, You Can Pray

Prayer is not something mysterious or esoteric or something that we learn how to do in school. Prayer is conversation. If we can talk, we can pray. Of course we can learn to pray better, just as we can learn to be better conversationalists. That, in fact, was Ignatius's intention in putting together his Spiritual Exercises. But the essential activity of prayer springs naturally from our humanity. It is a matter of conversing with a very good friend.

—David L. Fleming SJ, *What Is Ignatian Spirituality?*

Note "prayer springs naturally from our humanity." Prayer isn't abnormal. It's not a supernatural "spiritual" state. It's as natural as conversation.

Take some time today to converse with God as you would with "a very good friend."

September 19

Did You See That?

A fundamental perspective of St. Ignatius: In our spiritual life we ought to pray for greater awareness and attentiveness. Do we really experience the life around us, or does it blow by us at the fever pitch of progress? A simple starting point is to pay closer attention to our lives and the people and events that fill them. It is as if Ignatius is constantly prodding us saying, "Did you see that? Did you notice what you were feeling in that moment? Can you experience God in all of this? Ask God to show you."

—Patrick McGrath, SJ, "God, Dorothy Day, St. Ignatius, and the Examen of Conscience"

We must pay greater attention to what we have heard, so that we do not drift away from it.

—Hebrews 2:1

Lord, open my eyes that I may see you in the events of this day.

September 20

Indefinable "Somethings"

Discernment is rooted in the understanding that God is ever at work *in our lives—inviting, directing, guiding and drawing us into the fullness of life. Its central action is reflection on the ordinary events of our lives. It seeks to discover God's presence in these moments and to follow the direction and guidance he gives us through his grace. It is not the events themselves that are of interest, but rather the affective responses they evoke in us—feelings of joy, sorrow, peace, anxiety and all the indefinable "somethings" that arise and stir within us. It is precisely here that through faith we can discover God's direction and guidance in our lives.*

—Charles Jackson, SJ, "What is Discernment?", *New York Religious Life* blog

This is a crucial point in discernment—it's not the events that matter; it's our inner response to events.

What can you do to be more attentive to the "indefinable somethings" that stir within you?

September 21

What's Essential in the Spiritual Life

Above all remember that God looks for solid virtues in us, such as patience, humility, obedience, abnegation of your own will—that is, the good will to serve Him and our neighbor in Him. His providence allows us other devotions only insofar as He sees that they are useful to us. But since they are not essential, they do not make a man perfect when they abound, nor do they make him imperfect when they are absent.

—St. Ignatius Loyola, *The Letters of St. Ignatius of Loyola*,
William J. Young, SJ

Note that the "solid virtues" that Ignatius lists aren't flashy. Yet patience, humility, and the like are the essential things.

What "solid virtue" do you desire most? Talk to God about how to grow in this virtue.

September 22

Prayer Exercise

Over the next several days, practice listening. Listen to everything—traffic sounds, nature sounds, speaking sounds, and the sounds of peace and quiet. Try to listen with great attention for five or ten minutes every day.

Then, gradually tune in to God's voice. This voice will come through many of the sounds you have already been noticing. Don't say anything or ask for anything. Or if you do ask for something, may it be, "God, help me tune in to your voice."

—Vinita Hampton Wright, *Days of Deepening Friendship* blog

The voice of the LORD is over the waters;
the God of glory thunders,
the LORD, over mighty waters.
The voice of the LORD is powerful;
the voice of the LORD is full of majesty

—Psalm 29:3–4

Do the exercise.

September 23

Prayer for Generosity

Eternal Word, only begotten Son of God,
Teach me true generosity.
Teach me to serve you as you deserve.
To give without counting the cost.
To fight heedless of the wounds.
To labor without seeking rest.
To sacrifice myself without thought of any reward
Save the knowledge that I have done your will. Amen.

—St. Ignatius Loyola (attributed)

This well-known prayer was not written by Ignatius, but it is associated with him because it captures the spirit of the Ignatian attitude—generous, fearless, and eager to serve.

Pray the prayer several times slowly. Listen to what the Lord says to you.

September 24

The Conversational Apostle

Private spiritual conversation is an excellent method of helping our neighbor. It is the special quality of the conversational apostle to quietly and slowly win over his neighbor, to deal with him gently and light the flame of charity in his heart.

—Jerome Nadal, SJ, in *The Ignatian Tradition*, Kevin F. Burke, Eileen Burke-Sullivan, Phyllis Zagano

Conversation is an important idea in the Ignatian tradition. Ignatius greatly valued opportunities to engage others in quiet, personal discussion about the things that really matter, and he encouraged others to do the same.

Ask the Lord to give you opportunities to become a conversational apostle.

September 25

Heroic Virtue from Tiny Thorns

All our life is sown with tiny thorns that produce in our hearts a thousand involuntary movements of hatred, envy, fear, impatience, a thousand little fleeting disappointments, a thousand slight worries, a thousand disturbances that momentarily alter our peace of soul. For example, a word escapes that should not have been spoken. Or someone utters another that offends us. A child inconveniences you. A bore stops you. You don't like the weather. Your work is not going according to plan. A piece of furniture is broken. A dress is torn.

I know that these are not occasions for practicing very heroic virtue. But they would definitely be enough to acquire it if we really wished to.

—St. Claude de la Colombière, SJ, in *Voices of the Saints*, Bert Ghezzi

Do not lag in zeal, be ardent in spirit, serve the Lord. Rejoice in hope, be patient in suffering, persevere in prayer.

—Romans 12:11–12

Be mindful of the "tiny thorns" that will sting you today. Turn them into occasions for virtue.

September 26

Jesus Wants Us Free

Jesus wants neither selfish Christians, who follow their egos and do not speak with God, nor weak Christians, without will: "remote-controlled" Christians, incapable of creativity, who seek ever to connect with the will of another, and are not free. Jesus wants us free, and this freedom is to be found in the inner dialogue with God in conscience. If a Christian does not know how to talk with God, does not know how to listen to God in his own conscience, then he is not free.

—Pope Francis, Vatican Radio

For freedom Christ has set us free. Stand firm, therefore, and do not submit again to a yoke of slavery.

—Galatians 5:1

Ask the Lord: How am I not free? Make note of what he says.

September 27

An Active and Energetic Patience

Rule 321 [in the Spiritual Exercises] suggests an attitude of patience and hope:

"When one is in desolation, he should strive to persevere in patience. *This reacts against the vexations that have overtaken him. Let him consider, too, that* consolation will soon return." *(Emphasis added.)*

The patience referred to here is an active and energetic patience. This active patience helps us to see the desolation in perspective and keeps us confident that consolation will return in time. Ignatius actively persevered in patience as he contended with the desolation in concrete ways. The spirit of steadfast patience and hope prompted him to pray courageously for help and strength.

—Maureen Conroy, *The Discerning Heart*

Do not, therefore, abandon that confidence of yours; it brings a great reward. For you need endurance, so that when you have done the will of God, you may receive what was promised.

—Hebrews 10:35–36

Where do you need patience? How can your patience be more active and energetic?

September 28

Waiting on a Serious Choice

When we face a serious choice, we will try not to have made our minds up before we have to. We will be alert to having deep-seated prejudices and to making implied or even overt demands on God that the Lord crown our own self-originated choice with grace and happiness. On the contrary, we set ourselves to live this way: We will wait when alternatives are emerging. We will try not to favor one over the others until we are clear whether God is telling us something.

—Joseph Tetlow, SJ, *Choosing Christ in the World*

These are the classic principles of Ignatian decision making: alert to one's biases, patient, receptive to God's leading.

How can you apply these principles to a choice you are facing now or will face soon?

September 29

True Desire Is Fire in the Heart

A constant refrain running through the whole of the Exercises is the invitation to pray for what you desire. Ignatius believes that desire, as the deepest, most personal experience of grace, always reveals a person's true identity.

To discover what we deeply, truly desire forces us to wade into a swamp of needs, expectations, demands, casual wishes, moods, obligations, and much more. Your deepest, truest desire may coincide with one or another of these interior experiences but will always cut deeper into your heart than any of them. True desire is fire in the heart.

—George Aschenbrenner, SJ, *Stretched for Greater Glory*

Our deepest desires come from God. That means that when we know what we *really* want, we know what God wants too.

Spend some time today reflecting on your desires. What are your deepest desires? How have they changed?

September 30

God Is Trying to Catch Our Attention

God is always in conscious relationship with each one of us as our creator, our sustainer, dear father or dear mother, our brother, our savior, the Spirit who dwells in our hearts. Ignatius presupposes that at every moment of our existence God is communicating to us who God is, is trying to draw us into an awareness, a consciousness of the reality of who we are in God's sight. Whether we are aware of it or not, at every moment of our existence we are encountering God, Father, Son, and Holy Spirit, who is trying to catch our attention, trying to draw us into a reciprocal conscious relationship.

—William Barry, SJ, *Finding God in All Things*

My sheep hear my voice. I know them, and they follow me. I give them eternal life, and they will never perish. No one will snatch them out of my hand.

—John 10:27–28

How does God catch your attention? Look for him to show up again.

October 1

The Difference Between Preparing and Planning

In the first week of the Spiritual Exercises, Ignatius emphasizes the importance of preparing oneself to pray each day. In fact, he offers a few directives for prepatory prayer, praying about praying. Prepatory prayer is praying about that space, that opportunity, that moment that will shortly be upon me to be vulnerable to the Spirit of God. It is the petition for grace that I will faithfully respond. It is that vulnerability to whatever may be that differentiates preparing from planning.

—Lisa Kelly, *This Ignatian Life* blog

This is a most valuable insight—planning can shut us off from the spirit of God.

What do you do to prepare for prayer? How can you improve this?

October 2

When Feeling Low, Stand Pat

In the time of desolation we should never make any change, but remain firm and constant in the resolution and decision which guided us the day before the desolation, or in the decision to which we adhered in the preceding consolation. For just as in consolation the good spirit guides and counsels us, so in desolation the evil spirit guides and counsels. Following his counsels we can never find the way to a right decision.

—*The Spiritual Exercises* 318

It's often difficult to follow this advice. When we're feeling bad, our instinct is to do something—anything—to make things better. But that's the worst time to make a change.

Lord, I want to be guided only by you. Protect me from mistakes. Open my ears to hear your voice.

October 3

Do Everyday Things with a Great Heart

In following what St. Ignatius teaches us, the main element is to learn to be magnanimous. Magnanimity: this virtue of the great and the small which always makes us look at the horizon. What does being magnanimous mean? It means having a great heart, having greatness of mind; it means having great ideals, the wish to do great things in response to what God asks of us. [It means also] to do well the routine . . . daily actions, tasks, meetings with people—doing the little everyday things with a great heart open to God and to others.

—Pope Francis, *The Church of Mercy*

It will be very profitable for the one who is to go through the Exercises to enter upon them with magnanimity and generosity toward his Creator and Lord, and to offer Him his entire will and liberty.

—*The Spiritual Exercises* 5

Lord, I want to offer all to you and hold nothing back. Give me the grace to give you everything.

October 4

Jesus in the Checkout Line

When standing in line at the checkout I remind myself that the individual in front of me is the Christ and that the injunction to love her as I love myself is literally true. A little miracle happens: I not only love her but like her, and if her credit card is no good or her kohlrabi doesn't register, I don't get mad. By the time it is my turn to chat with the dark-eyed checkout girl from Nicaragua I am madly in love.

—Michael Leach, "The Face of Christ in the Checkout Line," *National Catholic Reporter*

Love is patient; love is kind; love is not envious or boastful or arrogant or rude. It does not insist on its own way; it is not irritable or resentful; it does not rejoice in wrongdoing, but rejoices in the truth. It bears all things, believes all things, hopes all things, endures all things.

—1 Corinthians 13:4–7

Today, when you are doing something tiresome like commuting or running errands, remember: "the individual in front of me is the Christ."

October 5

Christ in the Darkest Places

Is God present in all *things? Mathematicians and philosophers talk about a "limit case"—the point where a system breaks down, where we've taken an idea as far as it can go. Is there a limit case for finding God, a point beyond which God can't be found? I once read an angry comment to a blog post about finding God in all things: "tell that to the refugee mother in Africa trying to keep her kids from starving." But Christians say that God can be found even in the extreme circumstances of human suffering. Wherever we go, even in the darkest places, Christ is there too. He's gone there before us.*

—Jim Manney, *God Finds Us*

Who will separate us from the love of Christ? Will hardship, or distress, or persecution, or famine, or nakedness, or peril, or sword?

No, in all these things we are more than conquerors through him who loved us. For I am convinced that neither death, nor life, nor angels, nor rulers, nor things present, nor things to come, nor powers, nor height, nor depth, nor anything else in all creation, will be able to separate us from the love of God in Christ Jesus our Lord.

—Romans 8:35, 37–39

Thank you, Lord, for the great gift of your love and your presence, even in the hardest times and the darkest places.

October 6

The Devil's Strategy

How the evil spirit instructs his servants to lead people to ruin:

First they are to tempt them to covet riches that they may the more easily attain the empty honors of this world, and then come to overweening pride. The first step, then, will be riches, the second honor, the third pride. From these three steps the evil one leads to all other vices.

—*The Spiritual Exercises* 142

The evil one uses things that are not evil in themselves—material possessions, a concern for one's reputation, and self-regard. It's a clever progression, a slippery slope, an abuse of one thing leading to another.

Reflect on your attachments to money and material possessions. Do they occupy too much time and mental space?

October 7

The Benefits of Boring Prayer

Why does God lead us to ordinary times of praying, which we so quickly label as dry and boring?

God may be gently tilling the soil of your soul for some future harvest, preparing the ground for a bold insight or a deeper emotional experience to come.

God may use the times of dryness to heighten your sense of God's presence, so that you will be aware of that presence later in the day or week.

God may invite you to ordinary times to kindle deep desires and longings. In this case, restlessness is a good thing.

God may simply want to give you a rest after an intense experience of prayer. Enjoy the stillness and quiet.

Remember, in ordinary times of praying, we may feel that God is not there or not listening. To the contrary, God is there, but not as we imagine or have experienced in the past. Be faithful. God is always close.

—Kevin O'Brien, SJ, *The Ignatian Adventure*

Nevertheless I am continually with you;
  you hold my right hand.
You guide me with your counsel,
  and afterwards you will receive me with honor.
Whom have I in heaven but you?
  And there is nothing on earth that I desire other than you.
My flesh and my heart may fail,
  but God is the strength of my heart and my portion for ever.

—Psalm 73:23–26

Thank you, Lord, for guiding me, loving me, and being with me always.

October 8

A Greater Effort

The divine grace which Christ promises to those who have become discouraged is not intended to be a prop or a crutch to help them escape from their essential duties; rather, this grace is offered in order to inspire a greater effort. What grace gives is very real, but what it requires is first of all effort. All this is part of the divine paradox.

—Yves de Montcheuil, SJ, *Three Jesuits Speak*

The grace of God has appeared, bringing salvation to all, training us to renounce impiety and worldly passions, and in the present age to live lives that are self-controlled, upright, and godly.

—Titus 2:11–12

Pray for the grace to make the effort to tackle a chore or a difficulty that is gnawing at you.

October 9

A House for Everyone

"Father, I am a sinner; I have tremendous sins. How can I possibly feel part of the Church?" *Dear brother, dear sister, this is exactly what the Lord wants, that you say to him,* "Lord, here I am, with my sins." . . . *When you have the strength to say,* "I want to come home," *you will find the door open. God will come to meet you because he is always waiting for you—God is always waiting for you. God embraces you, kisses you, and celebrates. That is how the Lord is, that is how the tenderness of our heavenly Father is. The Lord wants us to belong to a Church that knows how to open her arms and welcome everyone, that is not a house for the few, but a house for everyone, where all can be renewed, transformed, sanctified by his love—the strongest and the weakest, sinners, the indifferent, those who feel discouraged or lost.*

—Pope Francis, *The Church of Mercy*

Greet one another with a kiss of love.

—1 Peter 5:14

How can you deliver this message of hope to someone who needs to hear it?

October 10

St. Francis Borgia, SJ

Today is the feast of St. Francis Borgia, SJ (1510–1572), who directed a great expansion of the Jesuits as the Society's third superior general. Francis was a Spanish nobleman, the Duke of Gandia, who gave up his titles and fortune when he entered the Jesuits after the death of his wife. As head of the Jesuits, he was especially attentive to the spiritual well-being of the men under his care.

He wrote:

When you pray, hear Mass, sit at table, engage in business and when at bedtime you remove your clothes—at all times crave that by the pain which he felt when he was stripped just before his crucifixion, he may strip us of our evil habits of mind. Thus, naked of earthly things, we may also embrace the cross.

—In *Voices of the Saints*, Bert Ghezzi

> And whatever you do, in word or deed, do everything in the name of the Lord Jesus, giving thanks to God the Father through him.
>
> —Colossians 3:17

When have you been most attentive to the presence of Christ in your everyday activities? What were the circumstances?

October 11

Ignatius's Optimism

Ignatius was close to being theologically and spiritually illiterate when he began his spiritual journey. He could find no reason why God singled him out. He was neither learned nor particularly pious and holy. Thus, he came to believe that God was calling everyone to intimacy and service. Jesuit spirituality has ever remained remarkably optimistic in its expectations of God's desire for closeness with everyone.

—William Barry, SJ, and Robert G. Doherty, SJ,
Contemplatives in Action

Ho, everyone who thirsts,
  come to the waters;
and you that have no money,
  come, buy and eat!
Come, buy wine and milk
  without money and without price.

—Isaiah 55:1

Spend some time giving thanks for the abundance of God's love and grace—so abundant that it sweeps up those "not particularly pious or holy."

October 12

Walter Ciszek, SJ

Walter Ciszek, SJ (1904–1984), an American Jesuit, was freed on this day in 1963 after twenty-three years in prison in the Soviet Union for doing clandestine missionary work. He described his experiences in two books, *With God in Russia* and *He Leadeth Me*. He described his prayer in prison:

Gradually too, I learned to purify my prayer and remove from it all the elements of self-seeking. I learned to pray for my interrogators, not so they would see things my way or come to the truth so that my ordeal would end, but because they, too, were children of God and human beings in need of his blessing and his daily grace. I learned to stop asking for more bread for myself, and instead to offer up all my sufferings, the pains of hunger that I felt, for the many others in the world and in Russia at that time who were enduring similar agony and even greater suffering.

—Walter Ciszek, SJ, *He Leadeth Me*

"Do not judge, and you will not be judged; do not condemn, and you will not be condemned. Forgive, and you will be forgiven."

—Luke 6:37

Reflect on the scripture verse above. What comes to mind?

October 13

Take, Lord, and Receive

Take, Lord, and receive all my liberty, my memory, my understanding, and my entire will, all that I have and possess. Thou hast given all to me. To Thee, O Lord, I return it. All is Thine, dispose of it wholly according to Thy will. Give me Thy love and Thy grace, for this is sufficient for me.

—*The Spiritual Exercises* 234

This is Ignatius's most famous prayer, called the *Suscipe* after the Latin word for "receive." It is the culmination of the Spiritual Exercises. In it we give God the only things he doesn't have—our freedom, our intellect, our memories, our very selves.

Pray the Suscipe.

October 14

Big Desires

Desire is the faculty which receives, so the bigger our desire is, the more we can receive. Our part in this life is to learn to want largely and earnestly enough to make us capable of the infinite rightness of God's kingdom. The more we try to tame and reduce ourselves and our desires and hopes, the more we deceive and distort ourselves. We are made for God and nothing less will really satisfy us.

—Simon Tugwell, OP, *The Beatitudes: Soundings in Christian Traditions*

Spirituality often has a modest tone: "My needs are few." Not Ignatian spirituality—the bigger the desire the better.

Ponder this idea: "Desire is the faculty which receives."

October 15

God Always Thinks Mercifully

God always thinks with mercy: do not forget this. God always thinks mercifully. He is the merciful Father! God thinks like the father waiting for the son and who goes to meet him when he spots him coming when he is still far off . . . What does this mean? That he went every day to see if his son was coming home: this is our merciful Father. It indicates that he was waiting for him with longing on the terrace of his house. God thinks like the Samaritan who did not pass by the unfortunate man, pitying him or looking at him from the other side of the road, but helped him without asking for anything in return—without asking whether he was a Jew, a pagan, or a Samaritan, whether he was rich or poor: he asked for nothing. He went to help him; God is like this. God thinks like the shepherd who lays down his life in order to defend and save his sheep.

—Pope Francis, *The Church of Mercy*

The Lord is gracious and merciful,
  slow to anger and abounding in steadfast love.
The Lord is good to all,
  and his compassion is over all that he has made.

—Psalm 145:8–9

How can you "think with mercy?"

October 16

"Find God in All Things"

Jerome Nadal, SJ wrote this about Ignatius:

In all things, actions, conversations, he felt and contemplated the presence of God and the attraction of spiritual things. He was a contemplative in action, something he expressed habitually in the words: "we must find God in all things."

—Jerome Nadal, SJ, in Maurice Giuliani, SJ *Finding God in All Things*

This is the classic formulation of the idea of finding God in all things—perhaps the central theme in Ignatian spirituality.

Holy Spirit, show me the presence of God in my life today—in large things and in small.

October 17

What Wasn't Said

In contemplation with the senses, Ignatius encourages prayer that puts us into the passage from scripture. We are instructed to use all our senses—hearing, sight, smell, touch, even taste. We are also instructed to contemplate what wasn't said, *that is, what isn't written in the Gospels. What would I have said? What side conversations might be going on? What would Jesus have said to me had I been there?*

Listen for what wasn't said then, but is being said to you now. In this is the message you need to hear.

—Lisa Kelly, *This Ignatian Life* blog

Call to me and I will answer you, and will tell you great and hidden things that you have not known.

—Jeremiah 33:3

Imagine what wasn't said at a familiar scene from the gospels. Scenes used in the Spiritual Exercises include the birth of Jesus, the calling of the disciples, and Jesus walking on the water of the Sea of Galilee.

October 18

The Man Who Lies Awake with Plans

It is none of my business to condemn a man who in this life lies awake with plans for adding to his buildings, his income, his estate, in the hope of leaving behind him a great name and reputation. But neither can I praise him; for, according to St. Paul, we ought to use the things of this world as though we used them not, and own them as though we owned them not—because the fashion of this world passes and in a moment is gone.

—St. Ignatius Loyola, *The Letters of St. Ignatius of Loyola*,
William J. Young, SJ

The appointed time has grown short; from now on, let even those who have wives be as though they had none, and those who mourn as though they were not mourning, and those who rejoice as though they were not rejoicing, and those who buy as though they had no possessions, and those who deal with the world as though they had no dealings with it. For the present form of this world is passing away.

—1 Corinthians 7:29–31

Reflect on your attachments, especially to time and money. How can you be more generous with them?

October 19

North American Martyrs

Today is the feast of the North American martyrs, eight French Jesuits who were tortured and killed in southern Ontario and upstate New York in the mid-seventeenth century during warfare between the Iroquois and Huron Indians. The Martyrs are St. Jean de Brébeuf, St. Noël Chabanel, St. Antoine Daniel, St. Charles Garnier, St. René Goupil, St. Isaac Jogues, St. Jean de Lalande, and St. Gabriel Lalemant.

Isaac Jogues is the best-known of the martyrs. He first arrived in New France in 1636. Several years later he was captured and enslaved by Mohawk Indians; he was tortured, and several of his fingers were cut off. He escaped and returned to France in 1642, but soon returned to New France. In 1646 he and Jean de LaLande were killed by Mohawks.

A month before he died, Isaac Jogues wrote this to a friend in France:

My confidence is placed in God who does not need our help for accomplishing his designs. Our single endeavor should be to give ourselves to the work and to be faithful to him.

> I am confident of this, that the one who began a good work among you will bring it to completion by the day of Jesus Christ.
>
> —Philippians 1:6

Reflect on the single-mindedness of St. Isaac Jogues and the other missionaries to New France. What can you learn from this?

October 20

Stick to the Business at Hand

Let us all persevere in the vocation to which God calls us. The enemy is wont to tempt those in the desert with thoughts of dealing with the neighbor and improving him, and to those who are helping the neighbor he will propose the great perfection of the desert and solitary life. Thus he lays hold of what is far off to prevent us from taking advantage of what is at hand.

—St. Ignatius Loyola, *The Letters of St. Ignatius of Loyola,* William J. Young, SJ

Temptation comes in an attractive package. One of Ignatius's rules for discernment is "It is a mark of the evil spirit to assume the appearance of an angel of light."

Take stock of your commitments. Are you inclined to change some of them? Why?

October 21

A Bit of Spiritual Psychology

When you come upon a strong, disordered attachment—an excessive eagerness to be admired and famous, for example—it can be freeing to pray against that attachment by praying not *to be admired and highly esteemed. This does not necessarily mean that you will never be admired again; but the nerve of the prideful sting is cut, and whatever fame and esteem come will be for God's glory and not your own. This is a bit of spiritual psychology that Ignatius offers.*

—George Aschenbrenner, SJ, *Stretched for Greater Glory*

Here's how Ignatius puts it in the meditation on humility in the Spiritual Exercises: "I desire and choose poverty with Christ poor, rather than riches; insults with Christ loaded with them, rather than honors; I desire to be accounted as worthless and a fool for Christ, rather than to be esteemed as wise and prudent in this world. So Christ was treated before me."

What's your reaction to this idea—to pray for poverty rather than riches, for dishonor rather than honor?

October 22

The Mindfulness Examen

Our examen teaches us, above all, to live in the present. The monk Thich Nhat Hanh points out that we humans are great at planning and willing to sacrifice today to save for cars and houses tomorrow, "But we have difficulty remembering that we are alive in the present moment, the only moment there is for us to be alive." So he exhorts us to the Buddhist practice of mindfulness, being fully and consciously aware (or mindful) of the present moment. The examen, by briefly pulling us out of our daily maelstrom, can help reorient us to the present. When we get it right, as Thich Nhat Hanh puts it, "Every breath we take, every step we make, can be filled with peace, joy, and serenity."

—Chris Lowney, *Heroic Living*

"Peace I leave with you; my peace I give to you. I do not give to you as the world gives. Do not let your hearts be troubled, and do not let them be afraid."

—John 14:27

Cultivate mindfulness by taking time out from your activities today to simply be aware of the present moment—"the only moment there is for us to be alive."

October 23

Love the Heretics

Anyone helping the heretics of this age must be careful to have great charity for them and to love them in truth, banishing from his soul all considerations which would tend to chill his esteem for them. We need to win their goodwill, so that they will love us and accord us a good place in their hearts. This can be done by speaking familiarly with them about matters we both share in common and avoiding any debate in which one side tries to put down the other. We must establish communion in what unites us before doing so in what might evince differences of opinion.

—St. Peter Faber, SJ, in *The Spiritual Writings of Pierre Favre: The Memoriale and Selected Letters and Instructions*

Faber isn't talking about simple good manners. He says that we must have real esteem and love for people with whom we are having serious disagreements.

Reflect on the magnitude of this challenge—to have genuine respect and admiration for people you're in conflict with.

October 24

God Needs to Hear Our Desires

Often we tell ourselves, or we are told, in an effort to quell our desires, to look at all the good we already have. We can be made to feel guilty and ungrateful for desiring what we want. But if we suppress our desires without being satisfied that God has heard us, we pull back from honesty with God. Often, the result for our relationship with God is polite distance or cool civility. Perhaps God cannot or will not grant what we want, but for the sake of the continued development of the relationship we need to keep letting God know our real desires until we are satisfied or have heard or felt some response.

—William Barry, SJ, *Letting God Come Close*

You have given him his heart's desire,
 and have not withheld the request of his lips.
For you meet him with rich blessings;
 you set a crown of fine gold on his head.

—Psalm 21:2–3

Tell God what's on your mind.

October 25

Good Prayer Means Good Listening

The good pray-er is above all a good listener. Prayer is dialogue; it is a personal encounter in love. When we communicate with someone we care about, we speak and we listen. But even our speaking is responsive: What we say depends upon what the other person has said to us. Otherwise we don't have real dialogue, but rather two monologues running along side by side.

—Thomas Green, SJ, *Opening to God*

Now the Lord came and stood there, calling as before, "Samuel! Samuel!" And Samuel said, "Speak, for your servant is listening."

—1 Samuel 3:10

Spend some time in prayer speaking to God, "as one friend to another," as Ignatius puts it.

October 26

A Cure for Dryness of Soul

As to that blindness or dryness of soul which you think you find in yourself, it may easily come from a lack of confidence, or faintheartedness and, consequently, can be cured by the contrary.

—St. Ignatius Loyola, *The Letters of St. Ignatius of Loyola*, William J. Young, SJ

Ignatius's remedy for spiritual dryness is boldness. Push ahead. Pray more. Act as if you had confidence.

How might boldness be part of the solution when you are experiencing spiritual dryness?

October 27

Christ Disguised

It is sometimes very difficult for us to find the presence of God in our lives. He will show up in places where we expect him to be, but he will also be "disguised." I tend to find Christ the easiest in the sick and the injured. It is in the everyday things, like life in the community, completing my studies, or a visit with my family where I can be blind to the presence of Christ.

So I ask you a question: where do you find Christ in your life? Do you see him in the everyday things? What about that person that you really find it difficult to love? Is Christ present in him or her?

—Jason Brauninger, SJ, *The Jesuit Post* blog

Joy, freedom, peace, wisdom—they all flow from our ability to answer the question: "Where do I find Christ in my life?"

Answer the question for yourself: Where do you find Christ in your life?

October 28

Ignatius's Mission

Inigo became convinced that experiencing God in a direct and immediate way was not a special favor reserved for a few select mystics. If God was willing to speak directly to a sinner like him, God would speak to anyone—anyone, at least, who was willing to take the time to be still, listen and pray. If people were willing to spend an extended period of time in solitude and prayer, daydreaming about Jesus the way he had at Loyola and Manresa, then he, Inigo, could help them experience God and learn God's will for them. This, he became convinced, was his mission from God: to help people experience God's presence and learn God's will by directing them in making the Spiritual Exercises.

—Ronald Modras, *Ignatian Humanism*

Ignatius's outlook was tremendously optimistic. God will speak to anyone—no matter how wounded or broken or sinful. All of us have the ability to hear God and share the work God is doing in the world.

Where do you need the confidence and optimism that Ignatius had? Ask God for it.

October 29

Respond to Christ *Now*

Our response to God occurs now. *We are not to be inhibited by our own weakness and failure. We are not to ponder our unworthiness. God is working in our lives* now *and we are to respond* now.

The Gospels show us Jesus entering into people's lives and inviting them to follow him—right from where they are, from boats and fishnets and from tax booths. He does not demand first that they run to the synagogue. Neither should we delay our response to God until we deal with our neuroses and character defects and our own sinful behaviors.

—David L. Fleming, SJ, *What Is Ignatian Spirituality?*

As he walked by the Sea of Galilee, he saw two brothers, Simon, who is called Peter, and Andrew his brother, casting a net into the lake—for they were fishermen. And he said to them, "Follow me, and I will make you fish for people." Immediately they left their nets and followed him.

—Matthew 4:18–20

Where do you hear Christ's call now, today? How can you answer this call?

October 30

St. Alphonsus Rodriguez, SJ

Today is the feast of St. Alphonsus Rodriguez, SJ (1533–1617). He was a humble lay brother who served as the doorkeeper at a Jesuit school in Majorca for forty-five years. He exerted great influence on Jesuits and lay people who came to know him, and was especially admired for his wisdom about finding joy in hardship. He wrote:

I must say, "What does it matter, my God, that I should endure for your love these small hardships? For you, Lord, endured so many great hardships for me." Amid the hardship and trial itself, I stimulate my heart with this exercise. Thus, I encourage myself to endure for love of the Lord who is before me, until I make what is bitter sweet.

Pray this prayer of St. Alphonsus Rodriguez:

Through your most holy passion and death,
I beg of you, Lord, to grant me a most holy life,
and a most complete death to all my vices and passions and self-love
and to grant me sight of your holy faith, hope, and charity.

October 31

God's Work of Art

We are God's work of art. Not all art is immediately pleasing. A civilized approach tries to widen one's range of appreciation to take in a greater variety of styles. So it is with people. If we limit ourselves to those immediately compatible, our circle of friends is going to be pretty limited. Once we make the effort to understand the worries and fears of others, we find life opening out in ways we never imagined.

—Peter Knott, SJ, *Thinking Faith*

Let mutual love continue. Do not neglect to show hospitality to strangers, for by doing that some have entertained angels without knowing it.

—Hebrews 13:1–2

What can you do to widen your circle of friends?

November 1

Martha and Mary Together

Prayer should be so directed that it augments and guides and gives spiritual relish to one's works, along with strength in the Lord, and so that the works will enhance prayer, giving it power and joy. In this way, Martha and Mary being joined together and assisting one another, not just a part of the Christian life is embraced.

—Jerome Nadal, SJ, in *The Ignatian Tradition*, Kevin F. Burke, Eileen Burke-Sullivan, Phyllis Zagano

The Ignatian outlook is both/and, not either/or. Prayer *and* work. Contemplation *and* action. God's grace *and* our effort.

Read and reflect on the story of Martha and Mary, Luke 10:38–42

November 2

Our Life Is a Response to His Call

Love Jesus Christ more and more! Our life is a response to his call, and you will be happy and will build your life well if you can answer this call. May you feel the Lord's presence in your life. He is close to each one of you as a companion, as a friend who knows how to help and understand you, who encourages you in difficult times and never abandons you. In prayer, in conversation with him, and in reading the Bible, you will discover that he is truly close. You will also learn to read God's signs in your life. He always speaks to us, also through the events of our time and our daily life; it is up to us to listen to him.

—Pope Francis, *The Church of Mercy*

To this end, we always pray for you, asking that our God will make you worthy of his call and will fulfill by his power every good resolve and work of faith, so that the name of our Lord Jesus may be glorified in you, and you in him.

—2 Thessalonians 1:11–12

Reflect on the pope's words, "Love Jesus Christ more and more."

November 3

False Supernaturalism

One of the most serious wounds that has been inflicted on the Church as a whole and on its individual members is false supernaturalism. All too often "God" has been found a very convenient alibi. Men have shrunk from their ordinary this-world responsibilities, either by a literal flight from them into the desert or the cloister, or by convincing themselves that "spiritual" values are so much more important than "natural" values.

—Thomas Corbishley, SJ, "False Supernaturalism," *IgnatianSpirituality.com*

Take action, for it is your duty, and we are with you; be strong, and do it.

—Ezra 10:4

What has been your experience with false supernaturalism? How do you handle tension between spiritual interests and everyday responsibilities?

November 4

A Saint Who Lives in Complete Activity

The Ignatian man ought to be a saint and he ought to live in complete activity. Previous spirituality opposed these two aspects. Activity seemed to be an obstacle to holiness, which was conceived as contemplation. The revolution accomplished by St. Ignatius showed that that which appeared to be an obstacle could become a means. To the heart filled with God, all things speak of Him.

—Jean Danielou, SJ, "The Ignatian Vision of the Universe and of Man," *Cross Currents*

"To the heart filled with God, all things speak of Him"—this is the secret of being a contemplative in action.

Lord, I want to see you everywhere. Show me how to love the people you love.

November 5

Stay Away from Motives

This is a comment on Annotation 22 in the Spiritual Exercises: "It is necessary to suppose that every good Christian is more ready to put a good interpretation on another's statement than to condemn it as false."

> *Stay away from motives. If you find yourself attacking somebody's motives, you are almost certainly violating Annotation 22.*
>
> *Attributing presumed motives to others shifts the discussion away from the* issue *and onto the* person*—and thus shifts it away from the question of truth as well. Moreover, attributing motives to others always strikes a false note for me because knowing someone's motives requires knowing their internal psychological states, a rather dubious proposition.*
>
> —Anthony Lusvardi, SJ, "Stay Away from Motives," *Whosoever Desires* blog

When you're tempted to question someone's motives, think about how irritating it is when someone questions your motives.

Are you staying away from questioning motives in your conflicts with other people?

November 6

A Prayer for Colleagues and Friends

May it please the supreme and divine Goodness
to give us all abundant grace
ever to know his most holy will
and perfectly to fulfill it.

—St. Ignatius Loyola, *The Letters of St. Ignatius of Loyola*, William J. Young, SJ

Ignatius ended many of his letters with this prayer. It expresses three characteristic Ignatian themes—confidence in God's grace, desire for discernment, and a commitment to action.

Pray the prayer, substituting me *for* us.

November 7

Beliefs Are Verified in Action

All religious beliefs are only verified in action. Indeed, "religious beliefs" that do not issue in complementary action are not religious beliefs at all; they are thoughts about the world, not beliefs. Someone may object: "But I am a sinner and often do not act according to my beliefs." That is true, but the very fact that you know that you are a sinner who does not act according to your beliefs shows that you have beliefs that must be verified in action.

—William Barry, SJ, in *Spirit, Style, Story: Essays Honoring John W. Padberg*, Thomas M. Lucas, SJ

This echoes one of Ignatius's most challenging claims—that "love ought to be shown in deeds rather than in words."

How will you verify your beliefs in action—today?

November 8

Confidence in God

I became conscious of that misery of mine which comes from my imperfections and my deficiencies above all in the conduct and affairs. In these moods of depression, this single consideration brought me some spiritual comfort: I saw that God was favorable to me. If I retain the certainty and the awareness of God's presence in me, he will make of me what I can and should be.

—St. Peter Faber, SJ, in *The Spiritual Writings of Pierre Favre: The Memoriale and Selected Letters and Instructions*

God is always favorable to us—a great message for people prone to depression (and everyone else as well).

Thank you, Lord, for your love and blessings to me. Make of me what I can be.

November 9

We Are All Part of the Great Work

A comment on Spiritual Exercises 362: "We should be more ready to approve and praise the orders, recommendations, and way of acting of our superiors than to find fault with them."

In today's world, this inclination to praise rather than blame and always assume the person is operating out of sincere motives, is sorely needed. We seem to have forgotten that we are all part of the Great Work, that all persons are an expression of God's loving presence—even those whose opinions are totally different than ours. They are still expressing some truth. And we need to look for the truth and build together on that foundation rather than focus on differences and tear each other apart.

—Pat Carter, "Ignatius of Loyola—Model for Lay Spirituality," storygroups.org

This principle sets a high standard; we don't just avoid unpleasantness, but actually praise and approve others. It means recognizing that other people often have better ideas than we do.

The next time your boss or teacher or pastor makes an important decision, praise them publicly.

November 10

A Task to Carry Out

Jesus did not leave us a list of truths to affirm, but a task to carry out. We must try to discern in our time and place how God wants us to live our lives in this world in tune with God's Spirit, the one divine action at work in this universe. This is what the discernment of spirits is all about. Followers of Jesus have been given a task to carry out and the means to do it. Impelled by God's Spirit, they must try to live in this world with the conviction that with the life, death, and resurrection of Jesus all the needful has been done, that God has won the victory he intends. Our task, therefore, is to follow the prompting of the Spirit, who has been poured out in our hearts, to follow the way of Jesus.

—William Barry, SJ, in *Spirit, Style, Story: Essays Honoring John W. Padberg*, Thomas M. Lucas, SJ

There are truths that are important to affirm, but Jesus didn't make that list. What Jesus said was "Follow me."

Thank you, Lord, for calling me to follow you. Show me the way.

November 11

God Always Surprises Us!

Newness often makes us fearful, including the newness God brings us, the newness God asks of us. We are like the apostles in the Gospel: often we would prefer to hold on to our own security, to stand in front of a tomb, to think about someone who has died, someone who ultimately lives on only as a memory, like the great historical figures from the past. Dear brothers and sisters, we are afraid of God's surprises! He always surprises us! The Lord is like that.

—Pope Francis, *The Church of Mercy*

Every valley shall be lifted up,
  and every mountain and hill be made low;
the uneven ground shall become level,
  and the rough places a plain.
Then the glory of the LORD shall be revealed.

—Isaiah 40:4–5

What new thing might the Lord be bringing into your life? Do you welcome it? Talk to the Lord about this.

November 12

Prayer for Detachment

I beg of you, my Lord, to remove anything which separates me from you, and you from me.

Remove anything that makes me unworthy of your sight, your control, your reprehension; of your speech and conversation, of your benevolence and love.

Cast from me every evil that stands in the way of my seeing you, hearing, tasting, savoring, and touching you; fearing and being mindful of you; knowing, trusting, loving, and possessing you; being conscious of your presence and, as far as may be, enjoying you. This is what I ask for myself and earnestly desire from you. Amen.

—St. Peter Faber, SJ, in *Hearts on Fire*, Michael Harter, SJ

Draw near to God, and he will draw near to you.

—James 4:8

Pray the prayer for detachment again slowly. What are the things that impede your walk with Christ?

November 13

St. Stanislaus Kostka, SJ

Today is the feast of St. Stanislaus Kostka, SJ (1550–1568). Young Stanislaus entered the Jesuits in the face of fierce opposition from his aristocratic family. He entered the Jesuit novitiate in Rome and died little more than a year later after demonstrating remarkable sanctity and spiritual maturity. He is a popular saint of Poland and of young people. Many religious institutions consider him a protector of their novitiates.

A classic expression of "finding God in all things" is attributed to him: "I find a heaven in the midst of saucepans and brooms."

> Let no one despise your youth, but set the believers an example in speech and conduct, in love, in faith, in purity.
>
> —1 Timothy 4:12

Pray this prayer by St. Claude de la Colombière, SJ:

O holy Heart of Jesus, dwell hidden in my heart,
so that I may live only in you and only for you,
so that, in the end, I may live with you eternally
in heaven.
Amen.

November 14

The Difference between Desire and Attachment

Attachment (what might be called disordered desire) always feels tumultuous, unsettling and lacking in peace. Deep desire has an element of peace in it and it pulls us generally forward rather than roiling uncontrollably. And they are very different in their effects: Clinging and attachment incapacitate. Deep desire energizes. Clinging and attachment lead only to pain and a feeling of incompleteness. Deep desire leads to satisfaction and peacefulness.

—Susan Stabile, *Creo en Dios!* blog

Ignatius writes, "the action of the good angel is delicate, gentle, delightful. It may be compared to a drop of water penetrating a sponge. The action of the evil spirit upon such souls is violent, noisy, and disturbing. It may be compared to a drop of water falling upon a stone."

Reflect on your desires and attachments. Which are tumultuous? Which bring peace and satisfaction?

November 15

St. Roque González, SJ

Today is the feast of St. Roque González, SJ (1576–1628), an innovative social activist who led the development of self-sustaining communities in Paraguay. González helped native people become self-sufficient and free at a time when Spanish conquistadors were brutalizing and enslaving them. He led the Jesuits who founded the "reductions," independent Indian village communities that excluded European settlers. The economy of the reductions made the Indians self-supporting by combining communal agriculture with private property holding. And the reductions had their own political structure that gave the natives a measure of freedom.

Gonzalez and two Jesuit companions were murdered by Indians in 1628. His work, and the opposition to it, was depicted in the award-winning 1986 movie, *The Mission.*

Pray this prayer of Pedro Arrupe, SJ:

Grant me, O Lord, to see everything now with new eyes,
to discern and test the spirits
that help me read the signs of the times,
to relish the things that are yours, and to communicate
them to others.
Give me the clarity of understanding that you gave
Ignatius.

November 16

The UCA Martyrs

Six Jesuits, their housekeeper, and her daughter were murdered on this day in 1989 at the Jesuit University of Central America in San Salvador, El Salvador. The UCA martyrs, as they are known, were assassinated by members of the Salvadoran army in order to stop their opposition to the government. Their murder was a turning point in the Salvadoran civil war. It increased international pressure on the regime, which soon made a peace agreement with the insurgents.

Dean Brackley, SJ, who moved to El Salvador after the massacre, said this of his fellow Jesuits:

They sought countless ways to unmask the lies that justified the pervasive injustice and the continuing violence, and they made constructive proposals for a just peace and a more humane social order. As a university of Christian inspiration, they felt compelled to serve the truth in this way. That is what got them killed.

—"The UCA Martyrs," *Thinking Faith* blog

Is not this the fast that I choose:
to loose the bonds of injustice,
to undo the thongs of the yoke,
to let the oppressed go free,
and to break every yoke?

—Isaiah 58:6

Prayer this prayer by Carlo Martini, SJ: "Lord, help me enter into that peace which consists in having put my life in your hands."

November 17

Hard Work Pays Off

Experience proves that in this life peace and satisfaction are had, not by the listless but by those who are fervent in God's service. And rightly so. For in the effort they make to overcome themselves and to rid themselves of self-love, they rid themselves of the roots of all passion and unrest. And with the acquirement of habits of virtue they naturally succeed in acting easily and cheerfully in accordance with these virtues.

—St. Ignatius Loyola, *The Letters of St. Ignatius of Loyola*, William J. Young, SJ

Here's a promise worth hanging on to: the work we do for God will form us in habits of virtue. Experience proves this, Ignatius says.

Use this promise to encourage someone to persevere in the hard work he or she is doing to overcome weaknesses.

November 18

The Creator Deals Directly with the Creature

There was one "doctrine" that was fundamental for [the early Jesuits], one that gave orientation to all their ministries and to the way they wanted to lead their own lives. It was the basic premise of the Exercises, even though it was buried unobtrusively in the fifteenth "Preliminary Observation": the Creator deals directly with the creature, and the creature deals directly with the Creator—heart to heart, one might say. Upon this teaching Jesuits based their more characteristic themes—indifference, discernment, and inner devotion, or consolation.

—John W. O'Malley, SJ, *The First Jesuits*

The same is true for us—everything flows from our connection to God. Without it, it's hard to sustain fruitful work and a joyful spirit.

Come, Holy Spirit. Fill my heart with knowledge of the wonder of God.

November 19

Imaginative Prayer

To follow Jesus we must know him, and we get to know him through our imagination. Imaginative Ignatian prayer teaches us things about Jesus that we would not learn through scripture study or theological reflection. It allows the person of Christ to penetrate into places that the intellect does not touch. It brings Jesus into our hearts.

—David L. Fleming, SJ, *What Is Ignatian Spirituality?*

Jesus took with him Peter and James and his brother John and led them up a high mountain, by themselves. And he was transfigured before them, and his face shone like the sun, and his clothes became dazzling white.

—Matthew 17:1–2

Apply your imagination to the Gospel account of the healing of the blind beggar near Jericho, Luke 18:35–43.

November 20

Asking God for Things

Asking God for favors is not imperfect prayer. When we beg God for sunny weather, or pray that our bursitis will go away, or pray for something more important such as international peace and justice, we pay a great compliment to God. This is an expression of "becoming as little children" which Jesus recommended, and honored. A child who comes to his parents and asks for things is paying them a big compliment. What is the child saying but, "You are good and can fill my needs. Please, may I have a candy bar?"

If the prayer of petition is made correctly, it says "God, you are everything: Creator, Sustainer, Divinizer, Forgiver, Merciful Lord of the Universe, Provident God of all, and I belong completely to You."

—Armand Nigro, SJ, "A Personal Response To God's Presence"

Ask and you will receive, so that your joy may be complete.

—John 16:24

Today ask for what you want, as Ignatius said—knowing that such a prayer gives great honor to God.

November 21

God Gets Us Moving

For most people, doing God's will means much intense action, and we have to be ready for that. The God of the Bible is almost always encountered in a command. Everywhere he says: "Go," "come," "do," etc. "Come follow me." God commands things we are supposed to do, and indicates responsibilities we have to take on. This is the way we encounter God in the Bible. We rarely find anyone encountering God by squatting and contemplating; God appears and gets us moving.

—Anthony de Mello, SJ, *Seek God Everywhere*

This echoes the Call of the King meditation in the Spiritual Exercises. Christ says "Let's go. Work alongside me. We will change the world."

Imagine Christ guiding you into the day to come, standing beside you as you work, with you as you interact with others.

November 22

Where Is It That You *Don't* Want to Go?

On the surface, we fun-seeking humans will do lots of things to avoid feeling bad. We shop. We eat. We yell. We procrastinate. Are they really leading us closer to God? Are they leading us closer to where and who we are called to be? Ignatius calls us to constantly go deeper, to be reflective and aware of the emptiness of those surface solutions. Where is it you don't *want to go? That's likely exactly where Ignatius would take you.*

—Lisa Kelly, *This Ignatian Life* blog

Where can I go from your spirit?
  Or where can I flee from your presence?
If I ascend to heaven, you are there;
  if I make my bed in Sheol, you are there.
If I take the wings of the morning
  and settle at the farthest limits of the sea,
even there your hand shall lead me,
  and your right hand shall hold me fast.

—Psalm 139:7–10

What are you avoiding?

November 23

Blessed Miguel Pro, SJ

Today is the feast of Blessed Miguel Pro, SJ (1891–1927). He worked secretly as a priest in Mexico at a time when public worship was banned and was executed by a firing squad in 1927, dying with his arms extended in the form of a cross, crying out "Viva Cristo Rey!" Pro was a lighthearted, cheerful man who did much to relieve the material suffering of the poor.

He wrote in a letter:

People give me valuable objects to raffle off, something worth ten pesos that I can sell for forty. Once I was walking along with a woman's purse that was quite cute (the purse not the woman) when I met a wealthy woman all dolled up.

"What do you have there?"

"A lady's purse worth twenty-five pesos. You can have it for fifty pesos which I beg you to send to such-and-such a family."

I see God's hand so palpably in everything that almost—almost I fear they won't kill me in these adventures. That will be a fiasco for me who sighs to go to heaven and start tossing off arpeggios on the guitar with my guardian angel.

Pray this prayer by Jean-Pierre Medaille, SJ:

Jesus, I want to unite my life to your life, my thoughts to your thoughts, my affections to your affections, my heart to your heart, my works to your works, my whole self to yourself, in order to become through this union more holy and more pleasing in the sight of your Father and in order to make my life more worthy of your grace and of the reward of eternity.

November 24

Rules for Imaginative Prayer

There are two absolute rules:

Never moralize or judge yourself.

Always respond from your heart and not from your head.

Neither rule is as easy as it sounds. Many of us carry judgmental attitudes toward ourselves from the past, and we are habitually critical of ourselves. We have also been taught to study the Word of God, and of course it's right to do this. But there is a time, too, for recognizing that our heads can never grasp the truths of God, and that our purpose in prayer is simply to respond, from our inmost depths, to what God is sharing with us of himself.

—Margaret Silf, *Inner Compass*

I pray that the God of our Lord Jesus Christ, the Father of glory, may give you a spirit of wisdom and revelation as you come to know him, so that, with the eyes of your heart enlightened, you may know what is the hope to which he has called you, what are the riches of his glorious inheritance among the saints.

—Ephesians 1:17–18

Take some time soon to pray imaginatively with one of your favorite passages from the Gospels.

November 25

How to Have a Civil Discussion

It is necessary to suppose that every good Christian is more ready to put a good interpretation on another's statement than to condemn it as false. If an orthodox construction cannot be put on a proposition, the one who made it should be asked how he understands it. If he is in error, he should be corrected with all kindness.

—*The Spiritual Exercises* 22

An excellent principle for daily life: If you hear something disturbing, assume the best and make sure you understand what's being said.

Apply this principle to a relationship, a work problem, or a family conflict.

November 26

Simplicity and Goodness Get the Upper Hand

Simplicity and goodness should eventually get the upper hand over our natural way of thinking. That is to say, though on a natural level we might think it right to be angry or depressed over something, nevertheless goodness and simplicity ought to put up with it.

—St. Peter Faber, SJ, in *The Spiritual Writings of Pierre Favre: The Memoriale and Selected Letters and Instructions*

It can't be any simpler: your anger might be perfectly justified; put up with the situation anyway.

Reflect on the situation that troubles you the most right now. Put it in God's hands. Pray for the grace to let it go.

November 27

Poverty, Insults, and Humility

Consider the address which Christ our Lord makes to all His servants and friends whom He sends on this enterprise, recommending to them to seek to help all, first by attracting them to the highest spiritual poverty, and should it please the Divine Majesty, and should He deign to choose them for it, even to actual poverty. Secondly, they should lead them to a desire for insults and contempt, for from these spring humility.

Hence, there will be three steps: the first, poverty as opposed to riches; the second insults or contempt as opposed to the honor of this world; the third, humility as opposed to pride. From these three steps, let them lead men to all other virtues.

—*The Spiritual Exercises* 146

This is Ignatius's understanding of how Christ leads his followers to virtue. It's a progression—poverty leading to indifference to one's reputation leading to humility. Note that none of these things is obviously attractive.

What is your inner response to this road to virtue? Is it appealing to you? Talk to the Lord about it.

November 28

St. Joseph Pignatelli, SJ

Today is the feast of St. Joseph Pignatelli, SJ (1737–1811), an important Jesuit leader who kept the spirit of the Society alive during the years of its suppression, 1773–1814. He was forbidden to work as a priest for many years and spent much of his life moving around Europe as he kept in contact with his dispersed brethren.

He wrote about patient endurance of troubles.

We were never without the sort of troubles which our lower nature would find it almost impossible to bear. So great is God's goodness, however, that he made all these things pleasant and gave us in addition great peace of mind and freedom from worry. All the fathers and brothers have very happy faces. They show themselves true sons of St. Ignatius and are guided by his spirit so that they find nothing distasteful when it is a question of obeying God's call.

—In *Whosoever Desires* blog

> [W]henever you face trials of any kind, consider it nothing but joy, because you know that the testing of your faith produces endurance; and let endurance have its full effect, so that you may be mature and complete, lacking in nothing.
>
> —James 1:2–4

Call to mind situations where are you called to exercise patience. Ask the Lord to stand beside you.

November 29

The Gateway to all Discernment

"Becoming aware" is the gateway to all discernment. How aware are we of our own interior spiritual experience? How often during the day do we advert to it? Do we ever consciously stop to become aware of what is stirring spiritually within? This is the first and most basic Ignatian teaching on discernment: be aware, seek to be sufficiently "within" so that what is stirring spiritually in our hearts becomes present to our consciousness.

—Timothy Gallagher, OMV, *The Discernment of Spirits*

We can cultivate a habit of awareness by praying the examen regularly.

Stop several times today and simply become aware of what is stirring in your heart. Ask the Lord what it means.

November 30

God Is One Who Labors

Consider how God works and labors for me in all creatures upon the face of the earth, that is, He conducts Himself as one who labors. Thus, in the heavens, the elements, the plants, the fruits, the cattle, etc., He gives being, conserves them, confers life and sensation, etc.

—*The Spiritual Exercises* 236

This is Ignatius's image of God—a busy, active God right *here*—in our everyday world, in our work and relationships—working to set things right. The last word—"etc."—invites us to consider for ourselves where we see God laboring.

What is your "etc."? Where do you see God at work in your life?

December 1

St. Edmund Campion, SJ

Today is the feast of St. Edmund Campion, SJ (1540–1581), a Jesuit who ministered to English Catholics during a time of persecution under Queen Elizabeth I. Campion was the most celebrated of the Catholic priests martyred for their faith under Elizabeth's persecution. His conversion to Catholicism caused a sensation at Oxford, where he was a brilliant young student. He joined the Jesuits in France and returned to England in 1580 to minister to Catholics in secret, knowing that this almost certainly meant that he would be executed.

Shortly before his death, he challenged the queen's privy council to give him a fair hearing and concluded with these words:

I have no more to say but to recommend your case and mine to Almighty God, the Searcher of Hearts, who sends us his grace, and sets us at accord before the day of payment, to the end we may at last be friends in heaven, when all injuries shall be forgotten.

—In *Edmund Campion: A Biography*, Richard Simpson

Pray this prayer by St. Clause de la Colombiere, SJ:

Jesus grant that I may die pursuing you, that I may die loving you, that I may die for the love of you.

December 2

A Heart for the Suffering and the Poor

What I would ask involves two things. First, that you look with your eyes and heart at these peoples who are suffering so much—some from poverty and hunger, others from oppression and repression. Then, because I am a Jesuit, I would bid you pray the colloquy of St. Ignatius from the first week of the Exercises before this crucified people, asking yourself: What have I done to crucify them? What am I doing to end their crucifixion? What should I do so that this people might rise from the dead?

—Ignacio Ellacuría, SJ, in *The Ignatian Tradition*, Kevin F. Burke, Eileen Burke-Sullivan, Phyllis Zagano

Ellacuría was one of the UCA martyrs—six Jesuits and two staff murdered in 1989 to stop their opposition to the oppressive government of El Salvador.

Pray the colloquy as Ellacuría suggests. What comes to mind?

December 3

St. Francis Xavier, SJ

Today is the feast of St. Francis Xavier, SJ (1506–1552). He was a companion of Ignatius's at the University of Paris and one of the founding members of the Society of Jesus. Xavier was one of the greatest of missionaries. He baptized thousands in India, the East Indies, Malacca, and Japan. His letters describing his missionary work circulated widely in Europe and had a great influence on the development of the Church's missionary outreach. Many men were drawn to the Jesuits by his example and became missionaries throughout the world.

Xavier loved and cherished his friends. He wrote:

For my own great comfort, and that I may have you constantly in mind, I have cut from your letters to me your names written in your own hand, and these I always carry about with me, together with the vow of profession which I made, to be my solace and refreshment.

—In *Voice of the Saints*, Bert Ghezzi

We, who are many, are one body in Christ, and individually we are members one of another.

—Romans 12:5

Think about your friends. What can you do to make your friendships stronger?

December 4

Stronger in Jesus

When the difficulties arrive, so do temptations. For example, the complaint: "Look what I have to deal with . . ." *A Christian who constantly complains, fails to be a good Christian: they become Mr. or Mrs. Whiner, no? Because they always complain about everything. Silence in endurance, silence in patience. That silence of Jesus: Jesus in His Passion did not speak much, only two or three necessary words . . . But it is not a sad silence: the silence of bearing the Cross is not a sad silence. It is painful, often very painful, but it is not sad. The heart is at peace. This journey of endurance helps us deepen Christian peace, it makes us stronger in Jesus.*

—Pope Francis, Vatican News Service

Do all things without murmuring and arguing, so that you may be blameless and innocent, children of God without blemish in the midst of a crooked and perverse generation, in which you shine like stars in the world.

—Philippians 2:14–15

Reflect on your "journey of endurance." When has it been most trying? How has it strengthened your faith?

December 5

The Glue That Binds it All Together

Trust is the glue that holds Ignatian spirituality together—trust of God, trust of the process of the Exercises, *trust in fellow Jesuits, trust in people's own experience of God, trust in God's presence in cultures, in learning, in art, in music, in technology. The litany of the objects of Ignatius's trust goes on and on. Ignatian spirituality trusts the world as a place where God dwells and labors and gathers all to himself in an act of forgiveness and in an act of blessing.*

—Howard Gray, SJ, "Ignatian Spirituality" in *An Ignatian Spirtuality Reader*, George W. Traub, SJ

What a joy it is to know that the world is a place where God dwells and labors, especially that he is found in our personal experience.

Review the last twenty-four hours. The last three days. The last week. Where did you experience God?

December 6

Jesus Is Our Fixed Point

If you ask a farmer how he ensures that he is plowing a straight furrow, he will give you this advice: Fix your eyes straight ahead, on some fixed point on the horizon—a tree perhaps—and keep moving steadily toward it. Don't watch the furrow. Just keep your hands on the plow and your eyes on that fixed point.

Jesus is our fixed point. He is at the head of each one of our personal lines of oxen teams.

—Margaret Silf, *Inner Compass*

Therefore, since we are surrounded by so great a cloud of witnesses, let us also lay aside every weight and the sin that clings so closely, and let us run with perseverance the race that is set before us, looking to Jesus the pioneer and perfecter of our faith, who for the sake of the joy that was set before him endured the cross, disregarding its shame, and has taken his seat at the right hand of the throne of God.

—Hebrews 12:1–2

Lord Jesus, I want to walk with you today. Make me aware of your continual presence. Let me see your work.

December 7

A Share in the Great Enterprise

God calls every one of us to share in a great enterprise. Ignatius tells us that no one is left out of God's invitation; young and old, lay, priest, religious, women, and men—all are called to share in God's plan. The lay person has a vocation, just as the religious and the priest has. The one thing that matters is to recognize our calling and respond to it faithfully.

—Peter-Hans Kolvenbach, SJ, "Message to Friends and Colleagues of the Society of Jesus"

"Go and tell John what you have seen and heard: the blind receive their sight, the lame walk, the lepers are cleansed, the deaf hear, the dead are raised, the poor have good news brought to them."

—Luke 7:22

Lord give me the one thing that matters: the grace to recognize your call and respond to it faithfully.

December 8

Jean-Pierre de Caussade, SJ

Jean-Pierre de Caussade, SJ, a French Jesuit spiritual director and preacher, died on this day in 1751. Caussade wrote *The Sacrament of the Present Moment*, a classic guide to prayer, in which he maintained that the present moment is a gift of God and that abandonment to it was a holy state.

He wrote:

Those who have abandoned themselves to God always lead mysterious lives and receive from him exceptional and miraculous gifts by means of the most ordinary, natural and chance experiences in which there appears to be nothing unusual. The simplest sermon, the most banal conversations, the least erudite books become a source of knowledge and wisdom to these souls by virtue of God's purpose. This is why they carefully pick up the crumbs which clever minds tread under foot, for to them everything is precious and a source of enrichment.

> I came to you in weakness and in fear and in much trembling. My speech and my proclamation were not with plausible words of wisdom, but with a demonstration of the Spirit and of power, so that your faith might rest not on human wisdom but on the power of God.
>
> —1 Corinthians 2:3–5

Where have you seen the presence of God in simple things—small details, commonplace ideas, humble events?

December 9

Something Is Always Happening

For Ignatius, something is always happening. It is of ultimate significance, for myself, for others, for the whole human race. What is happening is the drama of God's continuing creation of all reality and God's undying love for me, fully shown forth in Christ. How do I respond to that deepest reality? What is my active role in God's great work in Christ?

—John Padberg, SJ, "Saint Ignatius and the Bible," *Company* Magazine

When they had finished breakfast, Jesus said to Simon Peter, "Simon son of John, do you love me more than these?" He said to him, "Yes, Lord; you know that I love you." Jesus said to him, "Feed my lambs."

—John 21:15

Reflect on Padberg's question: what is my active role in God's great work in Christ?

December 10

For the Greater Glory of God

"For the greater glory of God." This was Ignatius's motto. He taught that it is important for us not just to do good things, but to do them for the right reasons. For it is certainly possible to perform seemingly good work for bad reasons: merely for money or fame, or to draw attention to ourselves, or to draw attention away from others, or to put off doing the less glamorous work we really should be doing. If we offer every task "for the greater glory of God," as Ignatius did, we will begin with the only worthy end in mind.

—Mike Aquilina and Kris Stubna, *Take Five: On-the-Job Meditations with St. Ignatius*

Notice the word *greater*. Many things give glory to God. What gives the *greater* glory?

Begin your day with the goal of making choices that will give God the greater glory.

December 11

A Personal Response to God's Presence

If prayer is a personal response to God's presence, then the beginning of prayer is to be aware of that presence, simply to acknowledge it, to be able to admit: "Yes, God my Father, You do love life into me. Yes, You love life and being into the things around me and into all that comes into my senses. You love talents and these longings into me." The focus is on God and what God does.

—Armand Nigro, SJ, "A Personal Response To God's Presence"

My eyes are ever towards the LORD,
  for he will pluck my feet out of the net.
Turn to me and be gracious to me,
  for I am lonely and afflicted.
Relieve the troubles of my heart,
  and bring me out of my distress.
Consider my affliction and my trouble,
  and forgive all my sins.

—Psalm 25:15–18

Begin your prayer today by simply being aware of God's presence. Pray the prayer in the reading, and begin with "Yes, God my Father, you do love life into me."

December 12

Avery Dulles, SJ

Avery Dulles, SJ (1918–2008), an influential theologian and prolific writer, died on this day in 2008. His conversion to Catholicism while a student at Harvard caused a stir because his family had prominent roles in the U.S. government. His father, great-grandfather, and great-uncle had served as Secretary of State. Another uncle was the director of the Central Intelligence Agency.

Dulles's aim as a theologian was to express Catholic tradition in language that speaks to contemporary culture. Pope John Paul II made him a cardinal in 2001.

Shortly after his conversion, Dulles wrote:

As the past recedes into obscurity, I watch it disappear without nostalgia. I recall it with difficulty and without delight. The man who looks toward Christ looks always forward, striving constantly to become more worthy of his divine Lover, hoping to draw a little closer to Him in this world and, after a little while, to be united with Him in everlastingness.

—On *Whosoever Desires* blog

As for me, I am already being poured out as a libation, and the time of my departure has come. I have fought the good fight, I have finished the race, I have kept the faith.

—2 Timothy 4:6–7

Lord, more than anything, I want to grow in love of you.

December 13

Offerings of Greater Value

Those who wish to give greater proof of their love, and to distinguish themselves in whatever concerns the service of the eternal King and the Lord of all, will not only offer themselves entirely for the work, but will act against their sensuality and carnal and worldly love, and make offerings of greater value and of more importance.

—*The Spiritual Exercises* 97

This paragraph from the Spiritual Exercises is the source of the idea of *magis*—the striving for *more*—the excellent, the best, the greatest. This openness to innovation and new ideas is one of the distinctive characteristics of Ignatian spirituality.

Where might the Lord be calling you to make "offerings of greater value?"

December 14

The World as God Sees It

Ignatius Loyola's Spiritual Exercises invite us to look at the world as God would see it. Why is this mental exercise important? Because facing facts about the world right now can help us see more clearly how we want to lead our civilization forward. What kind of world are we living in, where is it heading, and what part has each of us played in getting it there? Those big-picture questions typically remain unanswered because so many other concerns tunnel our vision. For an accurate perception of our world, we have to lift our heads a bit higher in order to see a bit farther.

—Chris Lowney, *Heroic Living*

To see the world as God sees it—this ambition is one of the purposes of the Spiritual Exercises.

Reflect on the circles you live in—family, workplace, community, parish, social networks? Ask God to help you see them as he does.

December 15

Always Look for the Good in People

Unless we look at a person and see the beauty there is in this person, we can contribute nothing to him. One does not help a person by discerning what is wrong, what is ugly, what is distorted. Christ looked at everyone he met, at the prostitute, at the thief, and saw the beauty hidden there. Perhaps it was distorted, perhaps damaged, but it was beauty none the less, and what he did was to call out this beauty.

Listen to other people, and whenever you discern something which sounds true, which is a revelation of harmony and beauty, emphasize it and help it to flower. Strengthen it and encourage it to live.

—Anthony Bloom, "Always Look for the Good in People"

I give you a new commandment, that you love one another. Just as I have loved you, you also should love one another.

—John 13:34

Apply this principle to a real person—a celebrity involved in a notorious scandal or crime, or perhaps someone you know personally who has behaved badly. Look for the good in him or her.

December 16

Knowledge Doesn't Satisfy the Heart

The one who explains to another the method and order of meditating or contemplating should narrate exactly the facts of the contemplation or meditation. Let him adhere to the points, and add only a short or summary explanation. The reason for this is that when one in meditating takes the solid foundation of facts, and goes over it and reflects on it for himself, he may find something that makes them a little clearer or better understood. This produces greater spiritual relish and fruit than if one giving the Exercises had explained and developed the meaning at great length. For it is not so much knowledge that fills and satisfies the soul, but the intimate understanding and relish of the truth.

—*The Spiritual Exercises* 2

Ignatius wanted the Spiritual Exercises to kindle a conversion of the heart, leading to a passionate commitment to the cause of Christ. That's why he wanted people to figure things out for themselves and not merely accept what they are told.

Consider a doctrine or other spiritual truth that puzzles you. Ask for an intimate understanding of it.

December 17

What Are Your Non-Negotiables?

Let's bring our "non-negotiables" to the surface. What assumptions underlie our thinking as we look at our choices? What vision of the "good life" do we hold to? What dream have we been pursuing? The point is not necessarily to put these things aside. The point is to become aware of the hold they have on us so that we can be free to choose as God would have us choose.

We will encounter fears as we probe our "non-negotiables." I'm afraid to do this because . . . my spouse won't like it . . . I might fail at that job . . . the grad school might turn me down . . . I'll have to take a pay cut . . . my friends will think I'm crazy . . . I'm comfortable with my life the way it is.

—J. Michael Sparough, SJ, *What's Your Decision?*

Concerns like these are not unreasonable; they need to be part of any major decision. But are they deal breakers, non-negotiables? Do they control your choices?

What are your "non-negotiables"? Examples: I must work for myself . . . live in this city . . . send my children to private schools.

December 18

A Prayer Exercise

Remember a time that you underwent a very significant and, perhaps, life-changing event. Remember the inner details and outer circumstances of the experience. Savor its richness, and relive it in your memory, feeling, imagination, heart, and mind. Notice God's presence. What were the circumstances of the experience, that is, were you by yourself, on a retreat, at a liturgy, in a group, or having a serious crisis in your life like Ignatius? What was God's presence like in the experience? What were some of your feelings, thoughts, and desires?

What differences did you notice within yourself as a result of this experience? Did any change take place in your life? Do you notice anything new happening in you now as you remember and relive the experience?

—Maureen Conroy, *The Discerning Heart*

I will call to mind the deeds of the LORD;
  I will remember your wonders of old.
I will meditate on all your work,
  and muse on your mighty deeds.

—Psalm 77:11–13

Do the prayer exercise.

December 19

Nothing Human Is Merely Human

The Ignatian ideal is that now we can have an experience of union and familiarity with God no matter the distractions of our work or banality of our lives. Here is the basis for finding God not only in all things but in the flurry of everyday life. Nothing human is merely human. No common labor is merely common. Classrooms, hospitals, and artists' studios are sacred spaces. No secular pursuit of science is merely secular. Like Ignatius after his experience at the Cardoner River, we see things differently. "The world is charged with the grandeur of God."

—Ronald Modras, *Ignatian Humanism*

You cause the grass to grow for the cattle,
  and plants for people to use,
to bring forth food from the earth,
and wine to gladden the human heart,
oil to make the face shine,
  and bread to strengthen the human heart.

—Psalm 104:14–15

Open my eyes to see your grandeur, Lord.

December 20

Something to Strive For

So let us simply strive to come closer to God in every way possible, happy feelings or not, and strive to avoid all that has the potential to take us farther from Him. For our spiritual life is all about union with God, and thus our consolation is in everything that helps make that happen.

—Abbot Joseph, *Making All Things New* blog

Note the simplicity of this, especially "happy feelings or not."

Ignatius writes, "Ask for an intimate knowledge of our Lord, who has become man for me, that I may love Him more and follow Him more closely."

December 21

St. Peter Canisius, SJ

Today is the feast of St. Peter Canisius, SJ (1521–1597). He joined the Jesuits soon after the Society's founding and became an important leader of the renewal of the Catholic faith in southern Germany. Peter worked at the height of the Protestant Reformation. He rejected attacks on Calvin and other Protestant leaders and counseled a moderate, conciliatory approach. He wrote:

It is a mistaken policy to behave in a contentious fashion and to start disputes about matters of belief with argumentative people who are disposed by their very natures to wrangling. Indeed, the fact of their being so constituted is a reason the more why such people should be attracted and won to the simplicity of the faith as much by example as by argument.

> But I say to you that listen, Love your enemies, do good to those who hate you, bless those who curse you, pray for those who abuse you.
>
> —Luke 6:27–28

How can you bring the simplicity of the faith to a tense relationship?

December 22

God in the Silence

In our prayer lives, God often speaks most clearly to us in moments when we can quiet our own minds and voices. Words can sometimes be more reflective of our own anxieties and concerns than of God's action. While prayerful words can be a beautiful mode of communication, they can also be distractions from fully placing ourselves in God's hands. Sometimes our words manifest our own limits. Silence makes room for the fullness of God's dynamic and healing power.

—Marina McCoy, "God in the Silence," *Dot Magis* blog

It is good that one should wait quietly
for the salvation of the LORD.

—Lamentations 3:26

Bring a particular concern into the silence with God. Listen to what God says.

December 23

Humility and Hubris

Humility says, "How can I serve you?" Hubris says, "Here's how you fix yourself."

—Greg Boyle, SJ, Homeboy Ministry, *America*

Rejoice with those who rejoice, weep with those who weep. Live in harmony with one another; do not be haughty, but associate with the lowly; do not claim to be wiser than you are.

—Romans 12:15–16

Identify a situation where a change of some kind is needed. How can you serve those involved?

December 24

What the Spiritual Exercises Are For

For just as taking a walk, journeying on foot, and running are bodily exercises, so we call Spiritual Exercises every way of preparing and disposing the soul to rid itself of all inordinate attachments, and, after their removal, of seeking and finding the will of God in the disposition of our life for the salvation of our soul.

—*The Spiritual Exercises* 1

This is how Ignatius describes the purpose of the Spiritual Exercises. It's a practical purpose: to identify and be free of disordered attachments so that we can joyfully serve God and other people.

Lord, free me from everything that hinders my service to you.

December 25

Seek the Grace of a Cheerful Heart

Let us seek the grace of a cheerful heart, an even temper, sweetness, gentleness, and brightness of mind, as walking in His light, and by His grace. Let us pray to Him to give us the spirit of ever-abundant, ever-springing love, which overpowers and sweeps away the vexations of life by its own richness and strength, and which above all things unites us to Him, Who is the fountain and the center of all mercy, loving-kindness, and joy.

—Blessed John Henry Newman, "Sermon for Christmas Day"

The angel said to them, "Do not be afraid; for see—I am bringing you good news of great joy for all the people: to you is born this day in the city of David a Savior, who is the Messiah, the Lord."

—Luke 2:10–11

Seek the grace of a cheerful heart on Christmas Day.

December 26

Grace Comes to Life in Our Deeds

"What have I done for Christ?"

"What am I doing for Christ?"

"What ought I to do for Christ?"

Return to these questions throughout the retreat. In one sense, they are not completely answerable during the retreat itself; we often lean into the answers as we continue our normal routines. By considering the questions, we realize how practical the Exercises are. Just as our sin is reflected in concrete decisions and actions, so, too, does grace come to life in choices and deeds for the love of Christ and others.

—Kevin O'Brien, SJ, *The Ignatian Adventure*

Those who look into the perfect law, the law of liberty, and persevere, being not hearers who forget but doers who act—they will be blessed in their doing.

—James 1:25

Ask and reflect on the questions: "What have I done for Christ? What am I doing for Christ? What ought I to do for Christ?"

December 27

How to Correct Others

For correction to be successful it will help much if the corrector has some authority, and acts with great affection, an affection that can be recognized. If either of these qualities is absent the correction will fail, that is, there will be no amendment. For this reason it would not be proper for everybody to undertake such correction.

—St. Ignatius Loyola, *The Letters of St. Ignatius of Loyola*, William J. Young, SJ

Ignatius is making a point about leadership and responsibility: Do we love the people we're responsible for? Is your relationship with them truly *personal*?

Think about Ignatius's observation: how can you deepen your affection for the people to whom you're connected?

December 28

Our Heart's Destiny

Thanks to your mercy, O Infinite God, I know something about you not only through concepts and words, but through experience. I have actually known you through living contact.

I have met you in joy and suffering, for you are the first and last experience of my life. Yes, really you yourself, not just a concept of you, not just the name which we ourselves have given to you!

You have descended upon me in water and the Spirit, in my baptism. Then my reason with its extravagant cleverness was still silent. Then, without asking me, you made yourself my poor heart's destiny.

—Karl Rahner, SJ, *Encounters with Silence*

We actually experience God; it's not just words and ideas. And God is our hearts' destiny—how wonderful is that?

Reread this prayer. Pray it slowly. Make note of what comes to mind.

December 29

What More Does God Want of Me?

The question we seek an answer for is "What more does God want of me?" More *is the* magis *of Ignatian spirituality—the aspiration to always grow in service for the greater glory of God.* Magis *has been described as the Jesuit "itch"—a restlessness in service, an ambition to maintain high standards of performance, a desire to conquer new frontiers. But it simply means* more. *We are loved by a God who loves without limit. We love him in return. What more can we do to love him?*

—David L. Fleming, SJ, *What Is Ignatian Spirituality?*

Whatever your task, put yourselves into it.

—Colossians 3:23

What are your feelings about this exhortation? Does it excite you? Puzzle you? Speak to God about it.

December 30

Get Outside Yourself

Get outside yourself—*Stop judging and start observing, observing, observing. Be aware of what is going on inside. Ignatius taught his companions to name what was going on inside and let it be what it is rather than trying to stomp it out or avoid it. He suggested seeing situations from multiple points of view, knowing that God is in all of them.*

—Lisa Kelly, *This Ignatian Life* blog

Be aware of what is going on inside. This is a key Ignatian principle, the foundation of discernment and freedom.

What have you observed about your inner life? What have you learned?

December 31

Trust in the Slow Work of God

Above all, trust in the slow work of God. We are, quite naturally, impatient in everything to reach the end without delay. We should like to skip the intermediate stages. We are impatient of being on the way to something unknown, something new. And yet it is the law of all progress that it is made by passing through some stage of instability—and that it may take a very long time

Your ideas mature gradually—let them grow, let them shape themselves, without undue haste. Don't try to force them on, as though you could be today what time (that is to say, grace and circumstances acting on your own good will) will make of you tomorrow.

Only God could say what this new spirit gradually forming within you will be. Give our Lord the benefit of believing that his hand is leading you, and accept the anxiety of feeling yourself in suspense and incomplete.

—Pierre Teilhard de Chardin, SJ, *Hymn of the Universe*

We end the year with words of encouragement and trust. We're on a journey. We can trust in the Lord, who is leading us, who is working within us, making us into something new. All will be well.

Spend some time today simply thanking God for his many blessings.

Acknowledgments

Every writer in this book has stirred and enlightened me in some way, but several of them are especially important to me. I am particularly grateful for the work of William A. Barry, SJ, the late David L. Fleming, SJ, Lisa Kelly, Chris Lowney, Tim Muldoon, and Ron Modras. They are my Ignatian luminaries.

I am indebted to many friends, colleagues, and companions in this Ignatian adventure, especially George Aschenbrenner, SJ, Paul Campbell, SJ, Steve Connor, Dennis Dillon, SJ, Joe Durepos, Bert Ghezzi, Ben Hawley, SJ, Rosemary Lane, Terry Locke, Tom McGrath, Becca Russo, and Vinita Wright.

Special thanks to Yvonne Micheletti, Beth Renaldi, and my wife Susan for their generous and meticulous work on this manuscript.

Copyright Acknowledgments

Scripture quotations are from New Revised Standard Version Bible: Catholic Edition, copyright © 1989, 1993 National Council of the Churches of Christ in the United States of America. Used by permission. All rights reserved.

Excerpts from *The Spiritual Exercises of St. Ignatius*, translated by Louis J. Puhl, SJ, copyright © 1951, Loyola Press, Chicago, IL. Used by permission. All rights reserved.

Excerpts from *America* magazine, New York, NY: "What Is Apostolic Spirituality?" by Brian McDermott, SJ, copyright © 2002; "The Chosen Path," by William Spohn, SJ, copyright © 2003; "Advent and Desire: A Meditation," by James Martin, SJ, copyright © 2010; "A Big Heart Open to God: The Exclusive Interview with Pope Francis," by Antonio Spadaro, SJ, copyright © 2013. Used with permission. All rights reserved.

Excerpts from *Take Five: On-the-Job Meditations with St. Ignatius*, copyright © 2008 Mike Aquiline and Kris Stubna, Our Sunday Visitor, Inc., Huntington, IN. www.osv.com, 1-800-348-2440. Used with permission. All rights reserved.

Excerpts from *Stretched for Greater Glory: What to Expect from the Spiritual Exercises*, by George Aschenbrenner, SJ, copyright © 2004 The Corporation of the Roman Catholic Clergymen, Loyola Press, Chicago, IL. Used by permission. All rights reserved.

Excerpts from *The Discerning Heart: Discovering a Personal God*, copyright © 1993 Maureen Conroy, RSM, Loyola Press, Chicago, IL. Used by permission. All rights reserved.

Excerpts from *Dot Magis* blog, the blog of Ignatianspirituality.com, copyright © 2009–2014 Loyola Press, Chicago, IL. Used by permission. All rights reserved.

Excerpts from *What Is Ignatian Spirituality?* Copyright © 2008 David L. Fleming, SJ, Loyola Press, Chicago, IL. Used by permission. All rights reserved.

Excerpts from *Letters of St. Ignatius of Loyola*, translated by William J. Young, SJ, copyright © 1959, Loyola Press, Chicago, IL. Used by permission. All rights reserved.

Excerpts from *This Ignation Life* blog, by Lisa Kelly, Ignatianlife.org, copyright © 2007–2014.

Excerpts from *Heroic Leadership: Best Practices from a 450-Year-Old Company that Changed the World*, copyright © 2003 Chris Lowney, Loyola Press, Chicago, IL. Used by permission. All rights reserved.

Excerpts from *Heroic Living: Discover Your Purpose and Change the World*, copyright © 2009 Chris Lowney, Loyola Press, Chicago, IL. Used by permission. All rights reserved.

Excerpts by Anthony de Mello, SJ, are from *Sadhana: A Way to God*, copyright © 1984; *Contact with God*, copyright © 2003; and *Seek God Everywhere*, copyright © 2010, Image Publishing, Colorado Springs, CO.

Excerpts from *Ignatian Humanism: A Dynamic Spirituality for the 21st Century*, copyright © 2004 Ronald Modras, Loyola Press, Chicago, IL. Used by permission. All rights reserved.

Excerpts from *God: The Oldest Question: A Fresh Look at Belief and Unbelief—and Why the Choice Matters*, copyright © 2000 William J. O'Malley, SJ, Loyola Press, Chicago, IL. Used by permission. All rights reserved.

Excerpts from *The Church of Mercy: A Vision for the Church*, by Pope Francis, copyright © 2014 Darton, Longman, & Todd, Ltd.; copyright © 2014 Periodici San Paolo s.r.l.; copyright © 2014 Edizioni San Paolo s.r.l.; copyright © 2014 Libreria Editrice Vaticana; Loyola Press, Chicago, IL. Used by permission. All rights reserved.

Experts from Vatican Radio, copyright © 2013, 2014, www.radiovaticana.va, Vatican City.

Excerpts from *Inner Compass: An Invitation to Ignatian Spirituality*, copyright © 1999 Margaret Silf, Loyola Press, Chicago, IL; first published in Great Britain by Darton, Longman, & Todd, Ltd. as *Landmarks: An Ignatian Journey*, copyright © 1998, Margaret Silf.

Excerpts from *What's Your Decision? How to Make Choices with Confidence and Clarity*, copyright © 2010 J. Michael Sparough, SJ, Tim Hipskind, SJ, and Loyola Press, Loyola Press, Chicago, IL. Used by permission. All rights reserved.

Excerpts from *Days of Deepening Friendship: For the Woman Who Wants Authentic Life with God*, copyright © 2009 Vinita Hampton Wright, Loyola Press, Chicago, IL. Used by permission. All rights reserved.

Every effort has been made to locate the copyright holders for the works used in this publication and to acknowledge the use of such works. Any mistakes or omissions will be corrected in the next printing of this book.

About the Author

Jim Manney is a popular author and editor of Ignatian spirituality books, including writing *What's Your Decision?*, *A Simple, Life-Changing Prayer*, and *God Finds Us*, and editing *What Is Ignatian Spirituality?* Manney lives in Ann Arbor, Michigan.

Continue the Conversation

If you enjoyed this book, then connect with Loyola Press to continue the conversation, engage with other readers, and find out about new and upcoming books from your favorite spiritual writers.

Visit us at **LoyolaPress.com** to create an account and register for our newsletters.

Or scan the code to the left with your smartphone.

Connect with us through:

Facebook facebook.com/loyolapress

Twitter twitter.com/loyolapress

YouTube youtube.com/loyolapress

Other Ignatian Titles

The Ignatian Adventure
Experiencing the Spiritual Exercises of St. Ignatius Loyola in Daily Life

$14.95 • Pb • 3577-1

God Finds Us
An Experience of the Spiritual Exercises of St. Ignatius Loyola

$9.95 • Pb • 3827-7

A Simple, Life-changing Prayer
Discovering the Power of St. Ignatius Loyola's Examen

$9.95 • Pb • 3535-1

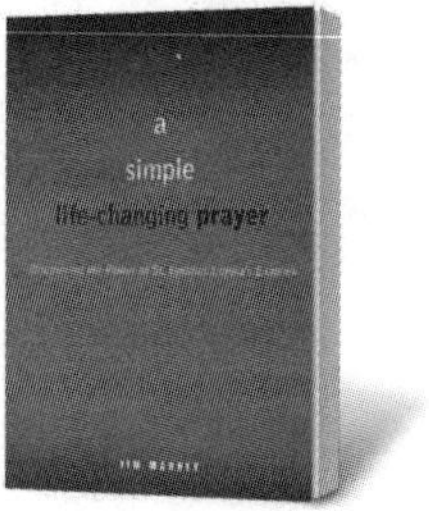

To order: call **800.621.1008**,
visit **www.loyolapress.com/store**,
or visit your local bookseller.